I’M THE WORST

"Clarkson's approachability and vulnerability will cause readers to reflect on their own lives and face their own brokenness. That can be scary to do, but reading Clarkson's work feels like talking to a friend who you can trust and who has been there before. Rather than feeling like a condemnation, the book reads like an encouragement. He handles sensitive topics with grace and compassion, and I would happily recommend this work for people at any point on their Christian journey."

—Zak Schmoll, PhD, founding editor of *An Unexpected Journal* and author of *Disability and the Problem of Evil*

"Any Christian will tell you that we are sinners in need of God's grace. But Nathan Clarkson, with heartbreaking vulnerability and deft use of research, makes that reality vividly personal and concrete. You will walk away with a deeper knowledge of how to accept God's love for yourself and extend it to others in an increasingly prideful and tribal world."

—Joseph Holmes, film critic, writer, and cohost of *The Overthinkers* podcast

"Honest. Raw. Relatable. Deeply transformative. *I'm the Worst* is the mirror held up in front of our faces that we all need right now. Nathan Clarkson speaks to every one of us who has ever felt like we could 'good kid' our way into love and belonging—every one of us who has thought we could use our perfectionism and overachievement like bright, blinking neon camouflage for all our many flaws, paradoxically blending in by forever standing out. He offers the go-to battle plan for taking back our lives one honest confession at a time. If the plank in your eye is starting to feel more like a pretty white-picket fence you keep putting up around a prison, Nathan is the trustworthy guide who will point you back to freedom. Read this excellent book!"

—Mary Marantz, best-selling author of *Underestimated* and host of *The Mary Marantz Show*

I'M THE WORST

how freedom is found in admitting our faults

Nathan Clarkson

I'm the Worst: How Freedom Is Found in Admitting Our Faults

Published by Kregel Publications, a division of Kregel Inc., 2450 Oak Industrial Dr. NE, Grand Rapids, MI 49505. www.kregel.com.

Published in association with the literary agency of Wolgemuth & Wilson.

The persons and events portrayed in this book have been used with permission. To protect the privacy of these individuals, some names and identifying details have been changed.

Cataloging-in-Publication data is available from the Library of Congress.

ISBN 978-0-8254-4987-1, print
ISBN 978-0-8254-4989-5, epub
ISBN 978-0-8254-4988-8, Kindle

Printed in the United States of America
26 27 28 29 30 31 32 33 34 35 / 5 4 3 2 1

To all the sinners, reprobates, and ragamuffins
on their way to becoming saints

This is a trustworthy saying, and everyone should accept it: "Christ Jesus came into the world to save sinners"—and I am the worst of them all.

—Saint Paul, 1 Timothy 1:15 (nlt)

Contents

Introduction: I'm the Worst / 11

Chapter 1: We're Not Good / 13
Chapter 2: But What About Them? / 20
Chapter 3: A Culture of Canceling / 29
Chapter 4: Hero Worship / 39
Chapter 5: Tribes Versus Communities / 48
Chapter 6: Forgive Them, for They Know Not What They Do / 57
Chapter 7: Canceling God / 69
Chapter 8: What Have I Done? / 82
Chapter 9: Death and Resurrection / 93
Chapter 10: What Now? / 105

Afterword: This Book Is for You / 114

Acknowledgments / 117
Notes / 119
Study Guide / 129
About the Author / 141

Introduction

I'M THE WORST

I'm the worst. I really am. You wouldn't know it from looking at me. I'm the son of well-known Christian leaders: My dad is a pastor, and my mom is a best-selling Christian writer. I'm a member of a beloved and idyllic family. I go to church. I've written best-selling Christian books. I make Christian movies. I have a podcast where I talk about faith. I study theology. I give to charity. I even post Scripture verses on my Instagram profile. But it's true—I'm the worst. Right beneath the surface of a good Christian guy lie three decades of bad choices, destructive addictions, cruel words, selfish actions, unfettered lusts, creeping envy, anger issues, constant doubt, prideful thoughts, and a seemingly endless list of fractured and failing parts that make me who I am: the worst. But it's okay. You're the worst too.

I used to believe I was good. It was easy when every pastor, friend, and book told me I was. Especially when they told me that all the bad in the world was over there, with the other people from the other tribe who voted, lived, and believed differently than me. And believing I was good was wonderful. I walked around the world with an assured sense of righteous superiority. I believed I was good . . . until I realized I wasn't.

It wasn't all at once—it was in a million little moments spanning a multitude of years, each pushing me ever closer to the realization that I was just as broken and desperately in need of forgiveness, help, and redemption as the rest of the world I had grown accustomed to looking down upon.

This was both a terrible and beautiful realization. The terrible part is that I had to look at myself honestly in the proverbial mirror. I had to accept all the darkness that had hid itself beneath the shiny exterior for so long and then reckon with the ramifications of what I had done and who I really was. But the beautiful part is that I was finally able to ask God for help and accept the freeing forgiveness and mercy he offered me, enabling us—my Creator and me—to pick up the broken pieces I had been ignoring for years and slowly put them back together.

Jesus said that "the truth will set you free" (John 8:32). He didn't say it will be particularly pleasant. But freedom makes it all worth it. By facing the truth of who we really are—warts, scars, and blemishes—we free ourselves from the pressure of keeping up the charade we've always known deep down is just a show, and we finally experience the true love and acceptance we've longed for that can only come from someone who sees and knows us completely.

So yes, I'm the worst, but so are you. You might not know it yet, but read on, and together we'll discover the life-changing, freeing act of accepting the reality that we're the worst.

Chapter 1

WE'RE NOT GOOD

I have been all things unholy. If God can work through me, He can work through anyone.

—Attributed to St. Francis of Assisi

I can remember the first time I truly realized I wasn't good. I was seventeen years old, living in a whirlwind of growing pains and youthful idiocy that clouded my brain with prideful delusions of grandeur and told me I knew better than the wisdom offered to me by my parents and pastors. Like so many boys, my first realization of my lack of goodness involved a girl. She was a cheerleader and the object of desire of all my friends, and for some reason she liked me. We lay on separate couches one Wednesday afternoon after she had come over to watch TV, and I asked her if she wanted to be my girlfriend. To my utter shock, she said yes. I had never so much as kissed a girl before, and here was a real-life young woman who agreed to go steady with me.

The next week was filled with holding hands at school, nonstop texts on my Nokia, and finally moving to the same couch while watching TV. One night, as I lay in bed texting with her after the world had gone to sleep except for just us two, a moment of adolescent desire overruled all the sermons my youth pastor had given, stating "nothing good happens after midnight," and we decided that she should come over and sneak through my window. I waited patiently and nervously. The twinges of apprehension that rushed through my body were soon extinguished by the excitement of meeting up with a pretty girl late at night.

After a gentle knock at my window, we lay on my bed. The next thirty minutes were filled with awkward teenage talking and touching, giggling and kissing, and doing things that teenagers do. Soon enough she crawled back through the window, leaving me alone with my thoughts. And while I should have been on cloud nine as she disappeared into the night, I didn't feel the light and fun feeling that the pop songs said I would feel after giving in to my desires. Instead I felt a sudden and heavy darkness fall over me, and with it the terrible realization that I wasn't good. In a moment everything had changed—I had changed. I had always been a good Christian kid, from a good Christian family, who didn't do things all those other sinners out there did, like meet up and make out with girls. But there I was, having to face the fact that I wasn't better than other people, I wasn't the person others thought I was, and I wasn't the good person I thought I was.

I look back at that night now and, while still cringing at the awkwardness, have to smile at the innocence in comparison to the darkness I've experienced in the decade and a half since. But that night, there in the midst of my naive understanding of the world, I realized for the first time that I wasn't as virtuous as I had always believed I was. I realized that it wasn't just the non-Christians, secular celebrities, and sinners out there who were at fault for the "bad" in the world—it was me too.

We broke up not long after, as I was unable to handle the guilt of having done something that, in my mind, excluded me from the title of "good." A couple of weeks later, I found her at youth group and, in a desperate attempt to assuage my mental turbulence, apologized profusely. She smiled, unfazed, and graciously granted me absolution. But still, I look back at that night and remember it as the first time I realized . . . I'm not good.

It's Them

It's no secret the world is a troubling and chaotic place to live during these modern times. Not a day goes by where we don't see another atrocity, tragedy, or dysfunction taking place in every corner of the world. We are all too familiar with the pervasive racism, sexism, poverty, sickness, violence, abuse, greed, bigotry, hate, and anger experienced and displayed by people around the world on an astonishingly regular basis. These affect us all and leave us longing for a better world than the one we currently inhabit—the one that doesn't seem to be making the progress we want it to. The good news, though, is that by watching the news, listening to culture critics, and reading comment sections, it seems we have figured out who's to blame . . .

Them.

You know, *them*. The other people from the other tribe, political persuasion, religion, gender, culture, financial status, or race. Our neighbors, parents, or pastors. They're to blame. *Obviously*. And this is a good and comforting thought. We've become skilled at identifying the people causing all the problems. And what a relief—it always happens to be the ones who aren't like us. While we might have to deal with the terrible realities of a broken world, it's at least nice to know that we're the good guys and they're the bad guys. The only problem is, what if that's not true? What if "they" are not the only ones to blame and instead "we" are?

No, It's Us

There's a great (though unverified) anecdote about the well-known writer G. K. Chesterton. Sometime in the early 1900s, *The London Times* requested essays from prominent writers and thinkers of the day who would respond to the prompt, "What is wrong with the world?" Important people and respected intellectuals from around the city began penning their lengthy and eloquent responses, no doubt detailing the faults of society, people, and government in their wordy displays of intellectualism. But one response stood out among them all. It said this to the question "What is wrong with the world?"

> Dear Sirs,
> I am.
> Yours, G. K. Chesterton[1]

In two words, Chesterton displayed both his pithy genius and the deep, difficult truth that none of us wants to face. The reality is that the real problem in the world is us. All of us. There isn't a person alive today who isn't filled with the same problems we spend our lives pointing out in others. A lot of time is spent analyzing, calling attention to, and pointing out all the ways others are failing—be it online, in the news, or in our homes and workplaces. Rarely does that external, critical gaze turn inward to the selfishness, rage, and despair living in our own hearts.

In a 2016 study conducted by the University of London, researchers found that the vast majority of people believe themselves to be not only "moral" but morally superior to a majority of others.[2] A 2021 OnePoll survey found that three in four people believe themselves to be "a fundamentally good person," and almost half believe that they are "better" than everyone else they know.[3] This is surprising but also entirely expected. We all want to believe we are good, and even more than that, most of us desire and believe ourselves to be better than others. And maybe those people who believed themselves to be better actually are fundamentally good people, but that entirely depends on what definition of "good" we use.

Jesus ran into this too. He lived in a time in which groups of powerful people had decided and proclaimed they were good—and had identified those who were not. The religious people of the day took great care to make it known just how good they were, often by pointing out and shaming those they proclaimed were not. They evidenced their goodness by outward displays of morality. They kept all the laws, observed all the religious rituals, and even wore the right clothes so as to fall under the definition of "good" they had created. But then Jesus, this young teacher from backwater Galilee who claimed to be the Son of God (John 10:22–42), started teaching an entirely new definition of what true goodness was and is, saying things like

> You have heard that it was said to those of old, "You shall not murder; and whoever murders will be liable to judgment." But I say to you that everyone who is angry with his brother will be liable to judgment; whoever insults his brother will be liable to the council; and whoever says, "You fool!" will be liable to the hell of fire. (Matthew 5:21–22 ESV)

and

> You have heard that it was said, "You shall not commit adultery." But I say to you that everyone who looks at a woman with lustful intent has already committed adultery with her in his heart. (Matthew 5:27–28 ESV)

All of a sudden, the playing field was leveled.

Goodness is not just what we do on the outside—it's how we live on the inside. It turned out that the God of the universe gave a definition of *goodness* that none of us could possibly reach—one that suddenly made everyone a part of the problem, not just the nonreligious or Samaritans or conservatives or liberals . . . all of us.

The Real Truth

An endless number of TV shows are based around a host detailing and mocking all the ways people from other groups are messing up the world. Nonstop news programs have pundits who systematically lay the blame for the ills of the world in the laps of the opposing political party. Countless sermons preached by pastors claim that the desperate condition of the world is the fault of unbelievers. Scores of YouTube videos posted by atheists proclaim the evils of religion. Innumerable podcasts are dedicated to picking apart both men and women in efforts to blame the other for their pain. An infinite supply of blogs, articles, and books scathingly critique whomever they deem at fault for the brokenness of the world. And we sit entranced by these voices as they subliminally assure us that *we* are good and *they* are not.

Even in our interpersonal relationships, we humans have an amazing ability to place blame on the "other." We blame our spouses for our failing marriages, our parents for our disappointing lives, our children for our broken relationships, our bosses for our unhappiness, our employees for our mistakes, and so forth. There's a comfort that comes from knowing that we're not one of the bad people, that the fracture in the world and in our lives isn't our fault, and that our hands are clean. But it's a comfort that blinds us to the uncomfortable truth that really we are *all* responsible for the darkness that exists in the world.

The very first story involving humans in Scripture is of a man and woman, Adam and Eve, who were created in God's own image and lived in paradise. But soon after being tempted by a serpent, they disobeyed God and ate a forbidden and deadly fruit. And what happened when Adam was caught? Did he realize the error of his ways, own up to his fault, and deal with the consequences? No. He instead looked for someone to blame—his wife. "It was the woman you gave me" (Genesis 3:12 NLT).

We are *all* responsible for the darkness that exists in the world.

Not much has changed in the few millennia since this story was written. We are a fallen people, each filled with the same selfishness, rage, and fracture as the person sitting across from us. But we have such a hard time admitting that. We long to be good. We each desire so deeply to be whole and beautiful. But we're not.

None of us are. And we never were. In children we can see that the selfish and cruel tendencies in the human heart are there from the beginning. Children almost instinctively lie to cover up their mistakes, hit their classmates in anger, and greedily take the biggest cookie, displaying the broken behavior and proclivities that exist in each of us and live in the world now. Anyone with a toddler will tell you about the intrinsic sin nature in humans, even tiny ones.

The words in Scripture written thousands of years ago by an ancient psalmist and quoted by the apostle Paul are still startlingly accurate about the condition of the human heart today: "No one is righteous—not even one" (Romans 3:10 NLT).

And that truth is what hit me that night in my bedroom as a teenager: "I'm not good." This realization hit me hard because I'd spent so much of my time examining other people and what they were doing wrong. I still do. I spend hours watching videos and scrolling through X, judging those I see as "the problem." I spend days thinking about the ways my family, friends, or colleagues fail, all while I excuse and ignore the brokenness that lives in me and that I act out in the world. I do this until I suddenly find I can't anymore because I am forced to look at my own choices.

In the coming pages, I'm going to explore this hard reality: The problem with the world isn't just "them"; it's also "us." I want us to discover why we are so adept at pointing fingers at everyone but ourselves, how we can overcome it, and if there's any hope for us and the world we live in.

> God looks down from heaven
>   on the entire human race;
> he looks to see if anyone is truly wise,
>   if anyone seeks God.
> But no, all have turned away;
>   all have become corrupt.
> No one does good,
>   not a single one!
>
> (Psalm 53:2–3 NLT)

Chapter 2

BUT WHAT ABOUT THEM?

Judging others makes us blind, whereas love is illuminating. By judging others we blind ourselves to our own evil and to the grace which others are just as entitled to as we are.

—Dietrich Bonhoeffer, *The Cost of Discipleship*

I escaped quietly out of the movie theater and into the cold night air of New York City. I was having a panic attack. *Really?* I thought. *Right now?*

I'd been at an invitation-only screening of a documentary detailing the dark and terrible life of a once-beloved and now-fallen spiritual figure. With popcorn in hand, I was ready for the intoxication that comes with seeing someone else get caught and feeling that much better about myself. But during the first thirty minutes, as the sordid details of this character played on the screen, I felt a growing sense of dread. Every scene revealed the perverse actions of someone who touted themselves as a "good" and "moral" person.

Before it began, the director had spoken about how important it was to expose these kinds of terrible people for who they really were: the bad guys. And while I heard whispers of agreement around me, the audience seemingly glad to be on the side of the good guys, I sat there with a wave of darkness about to crash over me. It came in the form of a question that I didn't have the answer to, and left me in a free fall of uncertainty: *Am I really the good guy?*

Of course, I was saddened and angered by the abusive, destructive actions taken by a charlatan who paraded around as a "man of God" while lying, cheating, and manipulating his way through life. And I tried to sit in righteous superiority to this obviously bad man. But try as I might, as I watched the film, I couldn't keep my attention on him and his sins. My brain kept pulling my gaze back to me and mine. The reality hit me. I write Christian books, like he did; I tell other people how to live, like he did; I portray myself as a good man of God, like he did; I post inspirational Bible verses on Instagram, like he did. At the same time, like him, I sin enormously, fall daily, hurt people deeply, lust carelessly, and have an entire broken part of myself I don't let the rest of the world see.

Watching this documentary about a man who looked like the good guy from the outside but was actually the bad guy all along made me evaluate my own life, reputation, and behind-the-scenes darkness. I sat there, sweat crawling down my face, and asked myself, *Am I the bad guy? What would people think of me if all my dark thoughts and unforgivable actions were on-screen for all to see?* I fled the theater.

My wife and I walked through the crisp New York night to the edge of Central Park, where we found a bench so I could catch my breath. We sat silently and looked out at the cars zooming down Madison Avenue, all unaware of my breakdown. I put my head in my hands and another wave of the all-too-familiar barrage of unwanted and uncontrollable thoughts crashed over me. I felt my wife's hand touch my back in an attempt to comfort me and pull me out of my head and back into the real world. But I couldn't see past the hurricane of accusations my own mind was hurling at me.

After a moment, she asked me what was going on.

"I'm not good," I finally said, trying to compress all my thoughts into one succinct sentence that could capture my myriad emotions.

She, of course, objected as she moved closer, laying her arm over my shoulder. An attractive couple walked by, the woman laughing at a joke the man told. I wished I could be them. *They must be good*, I thought. My wife pulled my face to hers and told me again how good she believed I was. And while that should have comforted me, it only made things worse, because my mind told me I had fooled her too.

"I'm not good, and I tell people I am," I said.

I thought of all the letters I had received since I had released my first book and made my first movie, letters from people who saw me as someone to look up to, to give them hope, letters from people asking me for advice on how to live a good spiritual life. *You're a fraud*, my mind whispered as we sat there in silence, my wife searching for the words to help me out of my spiral while I went over every detail of every mistake I had ever made. Mistakes that I was suddenly sure disqualified me from the title of "good." Mistakes that I felt made me a hypocrite to the countless people who looked at me as some sort of godly example. Mistakes that made me believe I was unworthy of both her and God's love. Mistakes that made me realize I wasn't as righteous as I once thought I was.

Comparison Confessions

We've all heard about the modern conundrum that has arisen in the past couple of decades when it comes to comparison on social media. We compare our bodies, our bank accounts, our accomplishments, and our authority, jealous of what we see. But one thing rarely talked about is the comparison that strikes even deeper than these surface-level metrics: our goodness. Which one of us hasn't scrolled through X threads, Instagram profiles, and Facebook posts, judging how wrong and bad others are while conversely feeling the rush of dopamine that comes with the assurance we are right, better, and good?[1] We look at scantily clad models and instantaneously feel holy because we would never post a picture of our bodies for attention like they do. We look at those richer than us in their cars, mansions, and name-brand clothes and feel morally humble, as if we are somehow inherently better for having less. We read the political posts and memes of those on the other side of the aisle and immediately feel the haughtiness of being so much more enlightened and ultimately better than they are for being a part of the "right" side.

Writers of the ages have addressed the judgment issue too—and have looked inward. Sixteen hundred years ago, a man from modern-day Algeria wrote an autobiography that changed the course of history. It was a book unlike any that had been seen before, and it still stands out as a rarity among the writings we see now. It is called *The Confessions of Saint Augustine*, and it consists of the author recounting his life and detailing all the ways he had failed and sinned. St. Augustine wrote this book as a personal journal, but somehow the brutal honesty with which he looked at himself, his faults, and his needs has touched the hearts and minds of countless readers for over a thousand years. I think this is partially because St. Augustine was brave enough to do what we all long for but fear—to look honestly at ourselves as a way to receive the grace and love we so desire. In *The Confessions of Saint Augustine*, he wrote, "Humankind is quite inquisitive about someone else's life, but quite lazy about correcting their own."[2]

His words still ring true today. This reality and human proclivity are no better exemplified than in the entire industry we've built around showing and exposing the embarrassing and private lives of celebrities: tabloids. In one form or another, tabloids have been around for over a century, but with the rise of digital media, we have perfected this practice right into a multibillion-dollar industry called "celebrity gossip."[3] This category of journalism lives off headlines like "Look How Bad This Actress Looks Without Makeup" and "So-and-So Was Caught Cheating on Their Spouse" and "See This Beloved Actor Be Mean to a Barista." But why? Why would so many of us spend so much of our time looking at the worst moments of other people? Perhaps it's for the same reason we scroll endlessly through social media and look at all the ways other people are worse than us—how they're dressed, how they act, what they eat, how they spend their money. Because something about looking at the faults, failures, and mistakes of others makes us feel better about, and even more able to ignore, our own.

In addition to the increase of judgmental attitudes fueled by exposure to social media and tabloid culture, another recent phenomenon has risen: Public figures gain notoriety, fame, respect, and success by bashing the bad guys. It seems whenever I turn on my TV or scroll through social media, the influencers and figures who get the most comments, views, and attention are the ones with the most vitriolic "hot takes" on other people and how they're messing up. I've noticed a recent trend of authors, speakers, leaders, and pastors who mold their entire message and career paths around criticizing, calling out, and lambasting the "other" team. In some way, shape, or form, every word they write or speak is to discredit, dissect, and denounce whomever they and their tribe have identified as the bad guys. They write strongly worded articles, give searing lectures, and post memes and statuses pointing out all the flaws and shortcomings of everyone's side and tribe but theirs. They do this because there is money to be made by positioning yourself as "the good guy" and assuring those on your side that they are the good guys, too, and that all the bad in the world is "over there." Their books become best sellers, their follower counts and likes blow up, and their bank accounts get bigger. And the thing is, they're often right in their assessment of the "others'" bad behavior. But the sad reality is that in doing this they may have become blind to their own bad behavior and may negatively influence others.

Our Own Darkness

I came across an Instagram meme the other day with a surprisingly deep and convicting amount of truth in just a few words, so much so that I stopped scrolling and looking at the faults of others to examine my own life and moral failures. It read, "Don't judge someone just because they sin differently than you do."[4]

I'm usually unaffected by the often trite and shallow quote posters that come across my phone screen, but this one struck me in an uncomfortable yet meaningful way. Like all of us, I want so badly to be one of the good guys. But I know deep down just how broken I am. To combat that uncomfortable and painful feeling, I look at the failures of others to make myself feel a little better about my own goodness. I congratulate myself for not being like them. In locking my literal and figurative gaze on the sins of others, I can ignore the very real and serious brokenness in me. But the longer I look at others and distract myself from my own sin, the larger my own cracks get, prohibiting me from taking care of the problems in my own life that will bring about disaster should they go unaddressed for too long.

Something about looking at the faults, failures, and mistakes of others makes us feel better about, and even more able to ignore, our own.

In Jesus's famous Sermon on the Mount in Matthew 7:1–5, he addressed the human proclivity to see the sins of others while ignoring our own:

> Do not judge, or you too will be judged. For in the same way you judge others, you will be judged, and with the measure you use, it will be measured to you.
>
> Why do you look at the speck of sawdust in your brother's eye and pay no attention to the plank in your own eye? How can you say to your brother, "Let me take the speck out of your eye," when all the time there is a plank in your own eye? You hypocrite, first take the plank out of your own eye, and then you will see clearly to remove the speck from your brother's eye.

Jesus knew the very real and human tendency not only to look judgmentally on others but to do so in an effort to ignore and abscond from our own faults. We all do it. It's almost second nature. As children, our first instinct when we get in trouble is to yell, "He started it!" in hopes that the ramifications of someone else's actions will erase ours. It's a human coping mechanism that we have developed over thousands of years to help us escape the realities of our own darkness. But with every new generation fixing their vision more firmly on the problems and faults of others while ignoring their own, we find ourselves further and further from allowing God to fix these harmful traits in ourselves.[5] According to Christian author Michael Hidalgo, "Maybe we cannot stop judging and punishing others because something about it feeds us, and our appetite is insatiable. When we stand as judge, jury and executioner over another, it gives us the feeling of being superior and righteous. And, let's be honest, the alternative just does not give us the same feeling."[6]

When I first moved to Hollywood with dreams of becoming an actor, I had images in my mind of all the great and heroic characters I would play. I wanted to play these characters because they were who I envisioned myself as—good, heroic. This is why it came as a shock that when I auditioned and booked roles in television and film, I found myself playing the bad guys. My first role in a major feature film was that of an ax-wielding, masked psychopath terrorizing the protagonists. Not exactly what I had pictured in my head when it came to the characters I thought I was made for. And that was just the beginning. Since then I've played criminals, killers, outlaws, addicts, abusers, and every other fictional, archetypal bad guy. In each of these roles there was a safe distance from the actual reality of their evil because they were surrounded by a made-up story and their bad deeds only existed in a fictional world.

But recently I was given a role in a TV show to portray a historical murderer who actually lived, breathed, and existed in our world. After years of playing fictional bad guys, it was a surprisingly jarring sensation to portray a person who had caused real and lasting damage in the world. In studying the character, I was first repulsed and disgusted by the actions a fellow human had taken in hurting others. However, as I uncovered more about his early life and the ways that others had inhumanely hurt, abused, and neglected him, I saw past his infamous shell of a murderer and felt my heart break for him as a human, for what had been done to him and what he had become. While the sadness and anger for what he had done to others remained, it was now mixed with a subtle sympathy for his humanity, which the rubble of a broken world had buried, creating the monster he became.

It made me evaluate my own perceived goodness. I wondered, *If I had experienced his story, would I be any better?* I'd like to think so and am happy to report I've never murdered anyone. At the same time, I have to reconcile with the real hate, anger, and darkness I harbor in my own mind and soul.

Our Reflection

There's a beautiful song that has stayed with me over a decade since its release: "John Wayne Gacy," by Sufjan Stevens. John Wayne Gacy was one of the most infamous serial killers of the twentieth century, convicted of murdering and raping over thirty people. Which makes him an odd subject for a beautiful song. The song is simple, with a single guitar and delicate piano beneath soft and haunting vocals that detail the life and murders of the monster who was John Wayne Gacy. Each verse explores the darkness and depravity of this man who embodied the fullness of evil in the world. But in the final verse, the artist shifts the focus from the infamous killer to himself, saying that he is just like Gacy, and if you were to look beneath the floorboards of the artist's heart, you'd find the secrets he has hidden, just like the bodies beneath the floorboards of Gacy's home.

This is a powerful piece of artwork not just because of the masterfully composed music and poetry but because the artist was strong enough to tear his gaze away from the sins of someone else, even a serial killer, and look at his own closet of skeletons.

We all live with bodies hidden beneath the floorboards of our hearts, souls, and minds. Skeletons of regret, dysfunction, and shame hidden from view from both the world and, more importantly, ourselves. They lie there out of sight, scratching at the wood beneath our feet. And to drown out the noise of our own personal destruction beneath the surface, we point and yell and expose the skeletons of our neighbors. But until we, like the artist, tear our gazes from other people and look beneath our own floorboards, we will never be free from the ghosts that haunt us.

But if we choose to stop scrolling through the shortcomings of others and turn off our phones, staring back at us in the glass is our reflection, the person we should've been looking at all along. To tear our gaze from the sins of others to look at our own brokenness is an act of strength and bravery.

> Why worry about a speck in your friend's eye when you have a log in your own? How can you think of saying, "Friend, let me help you get rid of that speck in your eye," when you can't see past the log in your own eye? Hypocrite! First get rid of the log in your own eye; then you will see well enough to deal with the speck in your friend's eye. (Luke 6:41–42 NLT)

Chapter 3

A CULTURE OF CANCELING

Charity means pardoning the unpardonable, or it is no virtue at all. Hope means hoping when things are hopeless, or it is no virtue at all. And faith means believing the incredible, or it is no virtue at all.

—G. K. CHESTERTON, *HERETICS*

In the classic Arthur Miller play-turned-movie *The Crucible*, we watch the origins of the story that gave us the all-too-well-known phrase "witch hunt." It is a fictional retelling of the events in 1690s New England that led to the public executions of over twenty-five innocent men, women, and children. It takes place in a small Puritan community led by religious men who—believing there to be witches in their midst—publicly accuse, convict, and brutally kill people based upon rumor and hearsay. The people of the small town, each worrying that they could be next, point fingers at others, accusing their own family and friends to avert the wrathful eye of the executioners. Once a place of community and acceptance, the town is suddenly flipped on its head. The rule of every man for himself takes over, and the only way to avoid condemnation is to condemn someone else.

In the final scene, John Proctor, played brilliantly by Daniel

Day-Lewis in the 1996 film adaptation, stands trial, facing execution on the false accusation of his lover. The court offers him a way out of execution should he only sign a document of guilt that states he consorted with the devil. But John Proctor doesn't sign it. As he's about to be killed, the heartless judge asks him why he won't just sign the document. Proctor turns to the angry mob and brutal jury and says,

> Because it is my name! Because I cannot have another in my life! Because I lie and sign myself to lies! Because I am not worth the dust on the feet of them that hang! How may I live without my name? I have given you my soul; leave me my name![1]

John Proctor would rather die than admit to an untruth about who he is. The religious witch-hunting Puritans were seeking to put to death not only bodies but also the reputations of those found guilty. This is something we are all too familiar with now, three hundred years after those witch hunts.

We'd all like to believe that as a society we have moved beyond these barbaric tendencies. But the difficult reality is that while we, thankfully, no longer have mobs with pitchforks and torches publicly killing people found guilty of being a witch, we still have mobs on social media publicly killing reputations of those we find guilty. We still practice this tradition of being quick to point our fingers at those around us out of fear that the accusing eyes of the moral mob may make us their next victim.

We haven't gotten rid of public executions—we've simply developed them into public cancellations.

We All Fall Short (Except . . . Me)

I've had this theory since I was a kid that if you walked up to any given stranger on the street or at a party—a pastor, priest, politician, or any person—and said, "I know what you've done," they would think of some memory, some moment, some awful decision they'd made, and shame would strike at their heart and mind. This theory is predicated on my belief that *all* of us carry in our memories heavy shame and deep regret for the things we've done and the people we've been. Sure, some mistakes may be bigger than others, but the human experience of regret is universal. The apostle Paul wrote, "All have sinned and fall short" (Romans 3:23). And I believe Jeremiah expressed what so many of us feel:

> I turned away from God,
>   but then I was sorry.
> I kicked myself for my stupidity!
>   I was thoroughly ashamed.
>   (Jeremiah 31:19 NLT)

But if this is such a universal reality—that all of us have messed up and done shameful things—why are we so fearful about admitting it, and why do we go to such lengths to hide it? If we all have a less-than-appealing portrait of ourselves, why do we hide it in the attic so no one can see?

Sometimes those portraits get hung back on the walls. I had just moved to Hollywood as a young actor with big dreams when a monumental cultural movement took place in the city. Toward the end of the 2010s, a phrase arose, along with a movement behind it: *cancel culture*.[2] The phrase described a new phenomenon in culture, which I witnessed firsthand, revolving around famous people being "found out" and expelled from public acceptance as recompense for their discovered "sins."

These sins were usually in the form of an off-color comment someone had said in a past interview, a decade-old insensitive tweet, a youthful mistake coming to light, some off-screen behavior captured on cell phone videos, or even a friendship with the wrong person. The movement started with good motives, as an attempt to hold people accountable for toxic behavior and destructive actions, but like most movements that gain speed quickly, it spun out of control. The thought behind it was that there were good people and bad people, and outing and canceling the bad people would leave us with the most moral good guys.

But the longer the cancel culture ball rolled, the more we discovered that maybe no one was blameless and everyone had fallen short of the cultural morality in some way, shape, or form. What was meant to only target the creeps and the corrupt started taking down long-adored figures, trusted voices, and beloved personalities. It even took down some of cancel culture's loudest supporters and creators. Suddenly no one was safe.

To combat the seemingly unstoppable mob sweeping through modern culture, many in Hollywood and Washington, DC, and every other corner of America took proactive measures to hide the bad stuff in their past. At the same time, they performatively displayed their morals by doing things like jumping on quasi-activist social media trends in hopes of avoiding their number being picked for the firing squad.[3]

Cancel culture had felt so good in the beginning. It allowed us to kick back and enjoy the show as the "bad" people were taken down. But in the matter of a few years, suddenly everyone found themselves looking down its barrel, scrambling to have it point at someone—anyone—else. The movement had started with the rich and famous but swiftly worked its way down to the "regular people" level, where average Joes and Janes found themselves losing friends for saying the wrong thing, family members for having the wrong political beliefs, and even jobs for uncovered past mistakes.

What cancel culture accomplished wasn't an intrinsic change of heart and betterment of the souls of society's individuals. Instead it simply made performers out of us all—it made us learn to act morally when in public view to avoid public consequences and win public prizes. But cancel culture ultimately did nothing to address or engage with the darkness we all live with in the shadows of our own minds and souls.

Preserve and Protect (Our Own Goodness)

In the 2010s, comedian Louis C.K. was on top of the world. He regularly appeared on every late-night show, sold out stadiums to devoted fans, and won awards for his comedy specials and TV shows. For a short time, he was considered to be the greatest living comedian.[4] Then in 2017 everything came crashing down. Shocking allegations were made, and behind-the-scenes behavior came to light in published articles appearing in almost every major US newspaper and online media outlet. And suddenly the beloved comic was ousted from public affection and forced to take the long walk of shame out of the spotlight and into the cell of cancellation. For a few years, he disappeared into the celebrity void. His name only came up in the context of cautionary tales and hushed whispers of denouncement.

Then in 2020 Louis emerged from the darkness with a new comedy special. In it he addressed his cancellation and told the audience how lucky they all were that their "thing," their messed-up parts and shameful actions, weren't laid bare before the entire world to see and judge.[5] Louis was pointing out an uncomfortable reality that while he paid the public price for his sins, most of us have not had to bear what it's like for the world to find out who we really are. Most of us will never have our most shameful and disgusting moments shown to the entire world. But that doesn't mean we don't all have them.

I'm glad when abuse is found out and people in power are held accountable for their destructive and abusive actions. This is a good and worthy practice. But I worry that in the process of joining a mob to cancel others for their sins, we forget the gravity and weight of our own.

It's interesting to look at the particular phrase given to this modern movement, "cancel culture," especially the appearance of the word *culture*, which according to *Collins Dictionary* means "the behaviors and beliefs characteristic of a particular social, ethnic, or age group."[6] It's a definition that encompasses all of us. Cancel culture describes an entire society that has made canceling people a way of life. We have made a lifestyle out of our obsession with the sins and shortcomings of others in an attempt to feel better about our own. This culture has made us into moralists who spend our time judging others, and performers who do everything we can to convince ourselves and others we're one of the good ones.

In the process of joining a mob to cancel others for their sins, we forget the gravity and weight of our own.

Cancel culture, while entirely secular, mimics a religious movement that took place in the American church throughout much of the twentieth century. Fundamentalism began as a reaction to the "lost" and "liberal" ways of the modern world.[7] Like cancel culture, the movement started with good intentions: to preserve morality and protect people from the corrosive effects of rampant sin that came with a new century. But like any movement based solely upon moral behavior, over the next fifty years, it produced a group of people steeped in self-righteousness, pride, performative morality, and hypocrisy (in my opinion, and that of many others).[8] Fundamentalism shaped some people into individuals who wore facades of "goodness" while ignoring the cancer of hate, abuse, and selfishness that lived in their souls. Many of the pastors who preached on Sundays about the dangers of dancing, drinking wine, and watching secular movies would eventually have their sordid affairs, sexual abuse, and debauchery that they engaged in on Saturday nights found out.[9]

Both the secular cancel culture and the religious Fundamentalist movement based their ideologies on moralism, an attempt to get humans to behave properly in their outward lives. But both ultimately failed to address the inner positions of the human heart. They both allowed people to learn the steps to a dance where you could *look good* and *look down* on those who stumbled. They both believed that behavior modification through shame was the answer to the world's ills. But both collapsed as a result of their failure to actually change souls.[10]

There's a psychological concept called "actor-observer bias," which describes the tendency for people to ascribe context, excuses, and valid reasons to their bad behavior, believing themselves to have good reason to act as they did, while at the same time offering only judgment to others guilty of the same sins.[11] This essentially means we believe our faults are the result of external and understandable reasons, while concurrently believing other people's faults are due to their internal depravity. We are constantly on the lookout for ways to justify what we've done so we can ignore the gravity of our own mistakes while simultaneously offering no such service in our estimation of other people's mistakes.

We'd so much rather examine and judge the faults of others than have to probe and deal with our own.

A Divine Perspective

Two thousand years ago, no one had heard of either cancel culture or the Fundamentalist movement, but even then Jesus was dealing with people who had created their own moralistic movement—the Pharisees. The Pharisees were religious officials obsessed with observing the moral law and looking good, while practicing quick judgment on any they identified as having fallen short. Time and time again, they had run-ins with Jesus and often tried to cancel Jesus himself by catching him acting outside the bounds of their invented cultural mores. The Pharisees deeply hated Jesus, whose teaching seemed diametrically opposed to their philosophy of performative morality. The Pharisees spent their days gazing at and dissecting the outward actions of other people, while Jesus gazed into people's souls. The Pharisees were quick to harsh judgment and expulsion of those they deemed "wrong," while Jesus spent his days offering redemption to the moral outcasts.

In a particularly tense interaction between Jesus and the Pharisees, Jesus said,

> What sorrow awaits you teachers of religious law and you Pharisees. Hypocrites! For you are like whitewashed tombs—beautiful on the outside but filled on the inside with dead people's bones and all sorts of impurity. Outwardly you look like righteous people, but inwardly your hearts are filled with hypocrisy and lawlessness. (Matthew 23:27–28 NLT)

I can only imagine the look on people's faces as this young prophet claiming to be God told an entire group of religious and self-righteous men that they were essentially painted coffins on the outside and filled with rotting flesh on the inside.

In John 8 is an infamous and beautiful story that has echoed through history and hearts since its telling. One day as Jesus prepared to teach in the temple courts, the Pharisees brought before him a woman who had been caught red-handed in the inexcusable act of sleeping with a married man. She was dragged half-clothed into the streets and brought into the temple courts to be judged and condemned. Perhaps the Pharisees towered over her with stones in their hands, ready to end her life for her unforgivable sin. In those days, adultery wasn't something that would simply get you on the cover of a tabloid—it was a crime punishable by death.

And as Jesus encountered this fateful moment, he acted in a way that was opposite to the mob rules of that time and echoes with relevance now, even two thousand years later. Instead of picking up a stone and joining the mob to bring about her punishment, he bent and wrote on the ground with his finger as the Pharisees demanded answers from him, trying to trap him and permanently cancel the sinful woman. Scripture doesn't tell us what he wrote, but many scholars have posited that it was the secret sins of the Pharisees about to stone the woman.[12] Jesus stood, and with one sentence he changed everything. "All right, but let the one who has never sinned throw the first stone!" (John 8:7 NLT).

Scripture tells us that one by one the Pharisees, who had just moments before been ready to kill a woman in righteous anger, slunk away, quite possibly as a result of having to see their own sins written on the ground they were about to spill someone else's blood upon.

When they had left, Jesus asked the woman,

> "Where are your accusers? Didn't even one of them condemn you?"
>
> "No, Lord," she said.
>
> And Jesus said, "Neither do I. Go and sin no more." (vv. 10–11 NLT)

He lifted the woman out of the dirt and told her to go, to be free, forgiven, restored, redeemed, to start a new life without being tied to her past, and to "sin no more" (v. 11 NLT).

The Pharisees were so caught up in both the glee of canceling Jesus and the pleasure of their own moral superiority, all they wanted was blood. But Jesus, knowing the brokenness on both sides, leveled the playing field and sought to bring restoration, not revenge, upon the woman whose failings had brought her to her knees in his presence.

Outward moralistic policing is human—it's as old as humanity itself. But Jesus offered us a new way, a divine perspective that isn't focused only on the outward behavior that needs to be modified but also on the inward condition of a soul that needs to be redeemed and transformed. In the Old Testament, God said, "The LORD doesn't see things the way you see them. People judge by outward appearance, but the LORD looks at the heart" (1 Samuel 16:7 NLT), giving us a picture for how we ought to look at both others and ourselves.

It's much easier to stand off to the side with the screaming moral mob and feel superior to those we see fail than to put down our stones and do the hard work of gazing inward and dealing with our own sick hearts in need of saving, our own thoughts, actions, and moments that make us eligible for cancellation. And the only perfectly moral being who has the right to order a cancellation on all of us, doesn't. Instead our Creator offers us a chance, love, and acceptance. But the only way we can begin the process of entering into redemption and grace is if we turn our gaze from the faults of others to our own fracture and need, which is a painful and difficult act but one that can bring beauty and freedom.

> Therefore, as God's chosen people, holy and dearly loved, clothe yourselves with compassion, kindness, humility, gentleness and patience. Bear with each other and forgive one another if any of you has a grievance against someone. Forgive as the Lord forgave you. And over all these virtues put on love, which binds them all together in perfect unity. (Colossians 3:12–14)

Chapter 4

HERO WORSHIP

You either die a hero or live long enough to see yourself become the villain.
—Aaron Eckhart as Harvey Dent, *The Dark Knight*

If you walked into my childhood room, you'd find yourself surrounded by four walls on which hang multiple posters of Superman. Each displays, in bright colors, an image of a ridiculously muscled figure shimmering in the sun as he flies through the air with his red cape waving in the wind behind him. These images filled my childhood imagination, as I was looking for the kind of man I wanted to grow up to be. In my heart I desired to be Superman, to image in my own life the courage, bravery, and greatness of the iconic American hero, who in my mind was worthy of adoration, even worship. What started out as physical imaging—"flying" around my house in a cape, defeating invisible foes who kept attacking the living room—turned into an internal imaging as I became a teen trying to act out the pure goodness of the hero on TV and in the pages of comic books. I wanted to be that flawless image of a hero that Superman represented to me. I held Superman up as a picture in my mind and heart as the greatest good, someone whose presence I emulated, followed, and put hope in.

But then I grew up. As I stepped out of childhood into early adulthood, the fantasy of Superman faded to the back of my mind. I stopped reading my comics and started reading books. I stopped watching superhero movies and started reading the news. I still had that desire for a great figure I could look to and praise. But I was now in need of a real-life, flesh-and-blood Superman. One who didn't just save the day in a fantastical world but offered me a vision of what a hero could look like in real life.

As the fantasy of Superman dwindled and my mind was in the market for a new hero, I began attending a megachurch led by a beloved and charismatic hero-like pastor. This preacher had become internationally famous for his winsome sermons, best-selling books, and powerful presence. He was handsome and funny, and he drew tens of thousands of people every week. And suddenly the space in my head once filled by a fictional comic book hero was occupied by a real-life "hero" behind a pulpit. This pastor satisfied my craving for a hero to look to. For a few years, as I became more and more involved in the church, I watched the pastor like I had watched Superman. Along with thousands of others, I saw the pastor as some kind of figure on which to place my aspirations and adorations, until the day it all shattered.

One morning I woke to the news that my pastor—the trusted and beloved leader of thousands, the man of God who graced the cover of glossy magazines, and the best-selling author of self-help books—had been caught in a hotel room with a male prostitute and a bag of crystal meth. On Sunday mornings he had been preaching purity and religion, which he had no intention of following on Friday nights. In that moment when I heard the news, and in the moments that followed, all the pictures I had in my mind, all the belief I had in heroes, and all the hope I had of them being figures I could look to for guidance, cracked, and I was left feeling foolish that I had ever believed that heroes existed. I sadly understood that heroes were either fantasy . . . or fake. And while I accepted this truth in my head, my heart still believed there was something, someone worthy of my adoration and praise. So I kept hunting for heroes.

We *Need* a Hero

Hero worship seems to be an intrinsic human inclination. Try as we might to be solely independent creatures, we can't resist the urge to put our hope in and give our praise to individuals we see as worthy recipients of our adoration. This starts young, with our worshiping our parents and wanting to be just like them, infallible figures of good. Then as we grow and individuate, that gaze of adoration often turns to fictional superheroes or princesses, whose images we see on screens and magazine pages and that we plaster our bedroom walls with. Then as we exit adolescence, we move from familial and fantastical heroes to embodied ones in the real world outside our homes. We look to actors, authors, politicians, pop stars, and pastors on whom we can place our hope, desire, and praise.

But what happens when our heroes fall, as they are so inevitably prone to do? We've just discussed the pervasive presence of cancel culture. In the past few decades, even some of the most beloved figures have fallen, and their metaphorical statues have been publicly torn down. Watching so many once-beloved "heroes" fall in what feels like one fell swoop, we might be ready to give up on hero worship altogether. But has the human race given up on heroes?

As it turns out, we haven't. As soon as one falls, we just begin our search for new ones. And there's all too many who are ready to step in and fill that position—politicians who promise a new world if you vote for them, celebrities who stand in spotlights vying for your praise, or pastors who offer health, wealth, and prosperity if you follow them. But what all of them have in common is the stated promise to satisfy our deep desire and need for a hero who can save the day and offer us an image to conform to.

Not long ago I was cast in *The Veil*, a movie where I played a member of one of the most infamous cults in history. The historically evil leader was being played by a famous movie star who brilliantly inhabited the role of this charismatic man, and a handful of fellow actors and I portrayed his followers. Over the two weeks of filming this movie, interestingly enough, most of our scenes were normal in nature—cult members going to church services, doing chores, eating together. That was, until the last day of filming, when we reenacted one of the most devastating scenes in recent historical memory—the mass suicide of the entire cult.

My role that day was to act as one of the cameramen in the cult who captured the awful display before taking the poison himself. The director yelled "Action," and we each played our roles, taking the pretend poison and slowly dying. We did this for multiple takes from various angles, each of us lying on the ground, pretending to be dead. At a moment when I knew the camera wouldn't see me, I opened my eyes to survey what I hadn't seen as I lay in the dirt with my eyes closed. It was shocking and, though fake, sent shivers down my spine and put a knot in my stomach. I looked out across the devastating scene to see dozens of men, women, and children lying lifeless on the ground.

On the drive home, back to civilization, bathed in the 405 freeway's streetlamps, I couldn't help but ask myself how anyone could actually be so deceived to do something that awful.

We've all heard of and maybe been obsessed with the phenomenon of cults. We've watched in the news and on Netflix documentaries the intriguing and shockingly consistent stories about these separatist communities led by charismatic leaders who draw people in with promises of utopia, only to end in devastating tragedy. Many of us remember stories during the nineties of the Branch Davidians, led by David Koresh just outside of Waco, Texas, which ended with an FBI raid that resulted in the deaths of more than seventy cult members and four ATF agents.[1] Or the Peoples Temple doomsday cult in the seventies, led by the infamous Jim Jones, who convinced or forced nine hundred people to take their own lives.[2] And who could forget the Manson family cult, who murdered multiple people in the sixties, including a movie star.[3] These are just a few of the countless stories we've watched about people being led into disastrous situations by a leader they believed to be a hero or even God himself.

But as we watch and read these stories on our screens and pages, we do so with a detached smugness that assures us we could never be led astray in the way that these poor souls were. We believe ourselves to be above and better than the characters in these tragic tales, assuming that only the mentally ill and broken could be sucked into the schemes of liars and frauds. But upon a closer look at these tragic stories, we find that the people in these destructive communities weren't just society's outcasts and troglodytes, but instead they often were normal, everyday people just like us: doctors, lawyers, moms and dads. But how could this be? How could sane, intelligent people so easily be led astray and into such devastation?

In a paper written by psychiatrist Robert J. Lifton titled "Cult Formation," he details the three defining factors to what we consider a "cult," the first being a

> charismatic leader, who increasingly becomes an object of worship as the general principles that may have originally sustained the group lose power. That is a living leader, who has no meaningful accountability and becomes the single most defining element of the group and its source of power and authority.[4]

The most consistent theme among every cult we've seen pop up in the last century, be it secular or religious, political or spiritual, is that without fail all of them have been organized by a charismatic central figure.[5] A hero, if you will, who drew each member in with the promise of fulfilling the deepest longings of the human heart: purpose, direction, safety, an explanation of reality, and a destiny. And while this definition was made to apply to that of leaders of destructive separatist cults, it's a strikingly accurate description of many of the notables we follow today in mainstream culture. And while many of us scoff at the suggestion that we could ever fall prey to the schemes we see played out in harrowing documentaries, we fail to see how vulnerable we all are to the power of a magnetic hero. Who among us hasn't looked at a cultural figure and placed in them our hope, trust, adoration, and faith?

This is not something we ought to shame ourselves for or attempt to rid ourselves of. This desire to be led by a shimmering figure is a feature of humanity, not a flaw. We have a God-given need to believe in a hero, to have an outside person not only give us what we want but tell us who we really are. This is a natural and good thing to need, look for, and desire, but as with any kind of love and affection, it can be misplaced and misused. Often the heroes we are most drawn to tell us the things about ourselves we most want to hear. It's another way we go about avoiding the reality of who we really are—broken and imperfect people—and most figures in this world are all too happy to reassure you of your goodness in exchange for your worship. But are they worthy of it?

We've seen over and over again since the start of the cancel culture phenomenon how many "heroes" have fallen. Too often someone we believed to be a great hope was revealed for who they were all along—a fractured and failure-prone human who was only ever able to imitate the hero we were made to look to.

Recently on a trip home, I walked into my old boyhood room and gazed at the walls covered with those Superman posters. I reminisced about the bright-eyed kid I once was, who would lie in bed and idolize the superhero on his wall, believing he could be that kind of hero depicted on the shiny cardstock, shimmering in the light and drawn with perfect lines. Like a demigod to be adored.

I was fully convinced in my heart that I could become—no, that I was—the hero who could save the world, until little by little life chipped away at my mind and soul and revealed the brokenness and flawed humanity underneath the idealistic image I had crafted for myself. I wanted to hold on to that ideal, that image. But unfortunately, life had taught me that neither I nor anyone else, in all our human brokenness, would ever be someone who could save anything, someone worthy of being worshiped. I had gone from seeing myself as Superman to realizing that all along I was the person in the story whom Superman had to save. And while humbling, it was the beginning of my understanding that this is a beautiful thing—not that I'm in need of saving, but that there is a Savior who can fill that role.

I had gone from seeing myself as Superman to realizing that all along I was the person in the story whom Superman had to save.

I will never be that image of Superman I wanted to be. In fact, I'm often the opposite. I'm the citizen hanging off a roof in need of help as a result of my and others' choices, but the beautiful truth is that there is a hero worthy of worship, in a way I could never be, who's flying to my rescue.

God-Shaped Hole

The late writer and thinker David Foster Wallace, in his commencement speech "This Is Water," given to the graduating class at Kenyon College in 2005, said,

> There is no such thing as not worshipping. Everybody worships. The only choice we get is what to worship. And the compelling reason for maybe choosing some sort of god or spiritual-type thing to worship—be it JC or Allah, be it YHWH or the Wiccan Mother Goddess, or the Four Noble Truths, or some inviolable set of ethical principles—is that pretty much anything else you worship will eat you alive.[6]

It's here Wallace is getting to the heart of the human's need to worship and the importance of what we choose to bestow that worship on, warning that if we aren't careful, we will be eaten alive if the object of our worship isn't strong enough to bear the weight of our eternal hope. The only person who can bear that weight is the one whom we were created by to give our worship to—God. Like the heroes of this world, God promises us direction, identity, understanding, and something beautiful to pour our praise into. But unlike the heroes of this world, God and his promises are true. There is no facade or mask or hidden fractures. God is wholly and completely worthy of our praise and big enough to hold it.

The old adage "There's a God-shaped hole in everyone's heart," while cliché, is true. We long for God, and for centuries we have been trying to satisfy that longing with poor imitations of people, politicians, celebrities, pastors, and cult leaders who are all too willing to take the role only he was made to fill. We have hoped to find another god who looks like us, who promises us the things we want, who assures us we are great, whom we can earn love from, and who tells us what we want to hear, instead of the God who is distinct from us, who gives us the things we need, who reveals our brokenness, who tells us the truth, and who loves us even though there's nothing we can do to deserve it. Worshiping this God is harder. It's more painful, as he shows us our brokenness; more difficult, as he asks for total devotion; and more uncomfortable, as he requires transformation. But it's better. So much better. This hero, God, will not fail and will not crack, and he is who he says he is.

We humans were made to worship something, made to look to a "hero," and there is an endless supply of people who will try to fill that space in our hearts by promising us the world. But all of them are just poor reflections of the only one who will actually fill that "God-shaped hole" in our hearts. While we tend toward the cheap imitations because they're easier, allowing the infinite and perfect God to fill that infinitely deep desire in our hearts is the only way our longing will ever be satisfied, the only way we will ever discover who we are and who we were created to be.

> In the beginning was the Word, and the Word was with God, and the Word was God. He was with God in the beginning. Through him all things were made; without him

> nothing was made that has been made. In him was life, and that life was the light of all mankind. The light shines in the darkness, and the darkness has not overcome it. (John 1:1–5)

Chapter 5

TRIBES VERSUS COMMUNITIES

Community is first of all a quality of the heart. It grows from the spiritual knowledge that we are alive not for ourselves but for one another. Community is the fruit of our capacity to make the interests of others more important than our own. The question, therefore, is not "How can we make community?" but "How can we develop and nurture giving hearts?"
—Henri Nouwen, *Bread for the Journey*

In the hilarious, heartbreaking, and even horrifying 2019 film *Jojo Rabbit,* from filmmaker Taika Waititi, we follow a young German boy, Jojo, during the end of World War II, as he navigates a landscape of growing up in a changing world while secluded in the protected bubble of Nazi Germany. Jojo has a vivid imagination and has created an imaginary friend to keep him company and help him make sense of the world around him. The only problem is, this imaginary friend is markedly different from that of the whimsical characters we've seen in other children's tales, like *Winnie the Pooh.* Jojo's imaginary friend is Adolf Hitler. Played brilliantly by Taika, Hitler is a charming amalgamation of the endless propaganda Jojo has been led to believe about the world.

Hitler is fun and kind to Jojo and is the embodiment of the propaganda that helps craft his understanding of the evil and inhuman enemy (the Jews) their country is fighting. Hitler corroborates the outlandish tales Jojo's school, newspapers, and friends have told Jojo about the Jews—that they have monstrous features and are out to hurt and steal and destroy all that Jojo loves. Jojo is all too willing to believe and go along with this narrative—that is, until he finds the pretty, young Jewish girl his mother is hiding in the attic. Suddenly all the fantasies that had been woven in Jojo's mind come undone upon encountering reality. As his relationship with the girl blooms, Jojo finds his destructive misconceptions unraveling. The lies that had been planted in his mind that could live and thrive in the abstract suddenly die when he is faced with a real human interaction with someone he had only imagined.[1]

I won't give away the powerful, painfully heartbreaking, yet hopeful ending, but this modern tale hits straight to the heart of something we all must face, lest the world be destroyed because of the fantasies we've created about those who aren't in our tribe.

Outward Versus Inward

We all have a deep desire to belong. This is a good and beautiful desire placed in our hearts by a God who created us to exist inside a community that loves, accepts, and celebrates us. A community that makes us not only feel safe but seen. And this natural human desire is something every group and movement has seized upon from the dawn of time until the modern age. Every nondenominational church in America covers their websites, church screens, and flyers with phrases like "you belong" or "welcome home," while preaching sermons on how to get "plugged in" to the promised community so you can "do life together."

Outside the church walls, you have groups like the LGBTQ+ movement calling itself a community, one that regularly holds events, gathers in bars, and marches in parades in an effort to celebrate its members. Even major brands have caught on to the power in the promise of community by utilizing taglines like Facebook's

"More together"; HSBC's "Together we thrive"; LinkedIn's "We're in it together"; and CBS's "Welcome home." Community is a basic human need, one that's rooted in spiritual and scientific realities. According to the Centers for Disease Control, lack of community creates loneliness, which significantly raises one's risk of stroke, dementia, depression, and even suicide and death.[2] In a *Psychology Today* piece titled "The Importance of Cultivating Community," licensed social worker Elizabeth Dixon says this in relation to the importance of community in a person's life: "We are relational beings in nature, and when we're isolated or detached from a community, our health and mental health can quickly take a toll. Life is hard enough on its own. We're not meant to go about it alone."[3]

But many people do go it alone today. More than ever before, people are dealing with the modern world's killing effect of isolation and loneliness. You'd think with the inventions of the internet and social media, the opposite would be true. But studies show the feelings of isolation and loneliness persist.[4] Social media seems to only be a Band-Aid on the deep cancer of loneliness that plagues us.

Then in 2020, a sudden and unseen worldwide tragedy struck, causing the loss of lives and leaving billions isolated and alone to greater degrees than we'd ever seen in human history, dramatically worsening an already dire problem. The monthslong lockdowns and shelter-at-home orders prevented many from getting the small amounts of human connection they'd mustered by going to church, meeting at a coffee shop, or seeing a movie. People were unable to connect to the outside world in any meaningful way, and loneliness and suicide rates grew even higher than they had been, leaving a greater vacuum of need in people's lives.[5] A 2023 American Psychological Association study found that while rates are dropping since the pandemic, loneliness remains a problem: 17 percent of US adults feel lonely "a lot of the day," and that number rises to 27 percent for those in low-income households and 24 percent for young adults.[6]

Community is a good thing, a thing we need. But with any felt need, we can attempt to fill that void with toxic imitations of what we actually long for. And in a desperate time, we often take desperate measures to find, keep, and protect whatever semblance of community we have, lest we face our greatest fear—being alone. This fear can cause us to act in destructive ways. Like someone dying of thirst who's willing to do almost anything to find, keep, and protect a drop of water, even if it's poisoned. The need for community in a world that's short on supply and heavy in demand has led us to find shelter not in open and supportive communities but in insular and antagonistic groups. Out of a psychology of fear brought on by an isolating world, we gravitate toward groups that salve that angst through telling us who we are by showing us who we're not. These groups exist in reaction to the existence of others and see outsiders as a threat that could ultimately leave us on our own in a scary and lonely world. This phenomenon has caused many former communities to become tribes. What's the difference between a community and a tribe?

We often take desperate measures to find, keep, and protect whatever semblance of community we have, lest we face our greatest fear—being alone.

Collins Dictionary defines *tribalism* as the "loyalties that people feel towards particular social groups and . . . the way these loyalties affect their behaviours and their attitudes towards others."[7]

In an article written by psychologist Arash Javanbakht, he describes tribalism and its effects:

> Tribalism is the biological loophole that many politicians have banked on for a long time: tapping into our fears and tribal instincts. Some examples are Nazism, the Ku Klux Klan, religious wars and the Dark Ages. The typical

> pattern is to give the other humans a different label than us, and say they are going to harm us or our resources, and to turn the other group into a concept.[8]

These definitions show us tribalism is a natural outcropping of a fear-based psychology that creates groups that are insular, reactionary, and antagonistic in nature. Tribalism seeks to win out over other groups or individuals it believes are threats to it. It is not self-sustaining but lives only in opposition and war with the "other."

Conversely, *Collins Dictionary*'s definition of *community* is this: "sharing common interests, work, identity, location, etc."[9]

And according to an article written by David M. Chavis and Kien Lee, community is

> both a feeling and a set of relationships among people. People form and maintain communities to meet common needs. Members of a community have a sense of trust, belonging, safety, and caring for each other. They have an individual and collective sense that they can, as part of that community, influence their environments and each other.[10]

Communities are formed out of a desire to accept, support, and welcome people who need a "place." Tribes are formed out of a defensive spirit in reaction to those identified as "the enemy." Communities are formed out of joy and love; tribes are formed out of fear and anger.[11] Community is a concept that's inward focused, looking to support and love its members. Tribalism is a concept that's outward focused, looking to defeat and destroy those who are not its members.

We see this played out in modern culture, from political and religious groups to sports teams' fans, all the way down to customers of Shake Shack versus In-N-Out Burger.

There's no better exemplification of this reality than the culture of X, formerly Twitter. Sometimes when my day's been too peaceful and lighthearted, I open my X account and take a peek at its goings-on. Immediately I am confronted with a cesspool of tribalistic attacks mimicking the brutal battles of warring tribes throughout history, where people lob spears of accusations from their X tribes to the neighboring tribes, who shoot back their arrows in the form of character assassination, condescension, and dehumanizing insults.

While the media is new, tribal wars are an ancient human tradition. But does it have to be this way? Is there a way to satiate our deep longing for a peaceful community without resorting to antagonistic tribalism?

Romans Versus Christians

Recently I moved into a new neighborhood and attended the local church. Admittedly it had been a while since I had gone to church; I had fallen out of the habit during the pandemic, after which followed a year and a half of traveling and moving, making it difficult to regularly attend services. The majority of my interaction with the organized religious community at that time was online, and I felt a twinge of trepidation at returning in person to a place that represented a group known for constant, contentious, and contemptuous fighting among figures, denominations, and traditions about minor theology, practices, and even clothing choices. This behavior is par for the course. If you look back through church history, you'll see tribalistic behavior insidiously weaving its coarse and discolored threads through the beautiful fabric of the church—with hangings, holy wars, and inquisitions being carried out in the name of God's will. But ultimately these acts, I believe, were done out of human fear.

So I stepped through the old wooden doors into a small sanctuary filled with half-empty pews covered in refracted sunlight shining through the large stained-glass window behind the altar. The image on the glass was Jesus with open arms, welcoming all who found themselves inside his house. As I did, I was suddenly reminded of the community God had created the church to be. My heart was put at ease throughout the service as we worshiped God together, confessed our sins, and took Communion. At the passing of the peace (when we greet one another), I was approached, in my back-row pew, by a line of people of different ages, races, and socioeconomic statuses who offered me a smile as they shook my hand. No one asked me what my theological stances were, I wasn't grilled about my past, and I wasn't judged for what I was wearing. I was simply offered a warm peace and welcome into a community that lived by the image of Jesus they had displayed on their wall.

God created us to live in a community that supports, loves, and welcomes us. Not one that lives in angst and anger or moves out of fear. Not one built with turrets and walls, but a community created with open doors and open arms.

Two thousand years ago when Jesus roamed the earth, there was no shortage of religious, governmental, and cultish tribes, each scared of the other and each living in a state of fear, as evidenced by their constant efforts to bring the other down. But throughout Jesus's life, he seemed altogether uninterested in forming a club, tribe, or cult in reaction to the groups that posed imminent threats, even the ones that eventually killed him. Instead Jesus formed a community of people and taught them to live and move without fear, to turn the other cheek when wronged, and to love their enemies (Matthew 5:38–39, 44; 10:28). Jesus envisioned a people who weren't so concerned with defending and attacking as they were with creating and dwelling. Jesus wasn't worried about the temporal perils of this world; his community was an eternal one that could never be broken by earthly threats. He was building an eternal kingdom—the kingdom of heaven—that couldn't be destroyed even by the mightiest of foes.

Because of this, the community he built was one that could exist not in reaction to or in defense against "the other" but instead from a place of love, joy, and freedom for any who joined in. This philosophy played out through the early church. When the Roman Empire brutally attacked the early Christians—throwing them to lions, burning them on stakes, and murdering men, women, and children—the church chose to be a community that didn't live in fear and didn't hide in the dark or fight back with equal violence. Instead they chose to give over to God their fears, anger, and bitterness at the hatred they experienced and continue following Jesus's example of forming a community of love, joy, and peace. Many Roman and religious leaders at the time, holding the philosophy of kill or be killed, believed this little group of peaceful God worshipers would eventually die out or be scattered in fear. And though Nero certainly tried to wipe out Christians, history shows that as a result of their refusal to play by the base instinct of human fear and anger, this ragtag little group went on to shape all of human history and become the most influential movement for good in the world.[12]

Angst Versus Joy

There are a couple of truths wrapped up in the words *angst* and *joy*: (1) The world is a crazy, chaotic, and sometimes cruel place for us to live (angst), and (2) we were made to long for and have a community of people in which we are safe, supported, and free (joy).

Understandably, when these realities combine, it can make us feel like we must find and become part of groups that promise us protection against the "other" who threatens us. The problem is that these groups perpetuate the "us versus them" or "kill or be killed" mentality that has caused some of the greatest tragedies in human history, and this mindset will ultimately lead us to live a life of fear and hate.

But there is another option, one that takes seriously the realities of the harsh world and our need to belong: the way of community, the kind that Jesus established in his time on earth. It eliminates the fear we so often feel and frees us to dwell not in angst-filled antagonism but in joy-filled peace. We were created to live and thrive among others, not to fear the "other." In order to address the root desire in our hearts and fulfill the longings in our minds and souls, we must not be pulled into or distracted by the tribes that exist only in *re*action to perceived external threats. We must instead keep our eyes focused on finding communities that live fully in *pro*-action to an internal joy—ones that stand with their arms and hearts open to any and all who long for lasting connection.

> They devoted themselves to the apostles' teaching and to fellowship, to the breaking of bread and to prayer. Everyone was filled with awe at the many wonders and signs performed by the apostles. All the believers were together and had everything in common. They sold property and possessions to give to anyone who had need. Every day they continued to meet together in the temple courts. They broke bread in their homes and ate together with glad and sincere hearts, praising God and enjoying the favor of all the people. And the Lord added to their number daily those who were being saved. (Acts 2:42–47)

Chapter 6

FORGIVE THEM, FOR THEY KNOW NOT WHAT THEY DO

We cannot change the past, but we can change our attitude toward it. Uproot guilt and plant forgiveness. Tear out arrogance and seed humility. Exchange love for hate—thereby, making the present comfortable and the future promising.

—Attributed to Maya Angelou

I remember the look in the eyes of a close friend as they waited anxiously for my reply. My gut was tight with a confusing mix of anger, affection, rage, and remorse. They had done something that had gone beyond the skin-deep offenses that a relationship could withstand and heal from, something that had stabbed through my skin to my bone, which now throbbed with a pain that wouldn't leave. I looked at their pleading face and felt stuck. I knew forgiveness was what I, as a good Christian, was supposed to offer freely. But the swell of hurt felt too great in my throat to allow the words to leave my mouth. Something in my heart and mind blocked me from letting this person off the hook. Somehow I couldn't, as it wouldn't erase what had taken place but would only shift the weight off their shoulders and onto mine. The silence in the air hung heavy as I turned away.

The Power of Forgiveness

There's an old story about a man who is sentenced to a cruel and heavy punishment of nineteen years of prison and hard labor for stealing a loaf of bread. During his time in prison, his heart becomes cold and dark, and a deep bitterness grows, numbing his spirit to the goodness in the world. Upon his release, having no one to turn to and not a penny to his name, he finds himself alone and in need. While wandering through a small town, the ex-convict comes in contact with an old priest, who, seeing the man's need, invites him to stay in his home. The priest feeds him, gives him a warm bed, and shows this hardened man warmth and grace. When night comes and the priest has gone to sleep, the criminal moves through the dark and steals the priest's valuable silver before sneaking out the back door. But no sooner does the man leave than he gets stopped by the police, who find the stolen silver in his pack. They shackle the man and drag him back to the priest's house in the middle of the night.

The priest emerges from his room to find the man whom he had shown such great generosity and love caught in the act of stealing. The police officers throw the bag of stolen silver on the ground in front of the man. He stands there, chained, head hung low, awaiting the merited condemnation that will see him behind bars for the rest of his life. A tense silence falls over the room as the police stand ready to drag the man away.

The priest grabs something off the table next to him and walks over to the captured thief. He lifts the man's chin so that their eyes meet, and he says, "You forgot the candlesticks." He explains to the police that the bag of silver was a gift and the man should be set free. Once the police leave, the man stands alone with the priest, in disbelief at the priest's forgiveness and grace. Emotion overtakes him at being given such lavish and unearned mercy, and then the priest says to him these powerful words: "My brother, you no longer belong to evil but to good. It is your soul that I buy from you. I withdraw it from black thoughts and the spirit of perdition, and I give it to God."[1]

In these words lies the reality that through the acts of giving and receiving forgiveness, a connection to God can be made, who ultimately has the power to mend our souls and stories. It's here at the moment of forgiveness that one of the most powerful tales of redemption ever written begins—*Les Misérables*, written by Victor Hugo. From this defining moment of experiencing unearned forgiveness, the thief Jean Valjean changes the entire trajectory of his story to one of redemption, where he then begins offering to others the same unmerited grace he received, changing the trajectory of their stories as well.

Les Misérables is one of the most well-known and beloved stories in history—with millions of books sold—brought to life in Tony Award–winning Broadway musical renditions and an Oscar Award–winning movie adaptation. This story has touched the hearts of millions because it is a powerful story of redemption through the act of mercy and forgiveness, something we all long for deep down.

Mercy and forgiveness have the power to change stories and redeem lives. We are fallen and broken people, and whether we know that consciously or subconsciously, we each have a deep desire buried in us to experience the redemptive touch of mercy. So why is it so hard to offer it? Why is it so difficult to let go of the anger and hatred in our hearts toward the "other," toward people who have done deep and real harm to us, toward people who don't deserve it? And honestly, why should we do so at all?

Justice Instead of Revenge

On a seemingly mundane evening in June 2015 at a historic Black church in Charleston, South Carolina, during a weekly Bible study, a young white supremacist shooter, filled with hate and anger, walked into the small gathering and opened fire, brutally killing nine innocent people. This incident rocked the entire nation and world as we watched in horror as the reports came across our TVs and computers. We couldn't comprehend how something so deeply heinous and violent could happen in such a peaceful place to such loving people. How could a fellow human being act in such a depraved and hateful way to the point he could coldly murder so many without thought or feeling? It was a question no one truly knew how to answer. It was another moment in our nation's long line of sad and terrible moments that brought us collectively to our knees.

A dark and disturbing shadow hung over the country for months leading up to the shooter's trial, where the nation awaited some sort of cathartic vengeance to be served for this man's heinous acts. As the shooter awaited his sentence, the families of the victims were allowed to stand and face him to say their piece to the monster who had taken everything from them. But in that moment, when these individuals had every right to condemn and unleash vitriolic hate on this depraved man, they did something so unspeakably beautiful that its brilliance outshined the act of destruction he had caused. In some of the most moving acts of forgiveness, one by one the victims' family members took the stand and forgave him. A hush of awe fell over the country, and the video of their divine acts spread across the world. In a moving monologue with strength-filled tears, one of the family members, Nadine Collier, said this to the shooter: "I forgive you and have mercy on your soul. It hurts me, it hurts a lot of people but God forgive you and I forgive you."[2]

Her words rang out around the world, causing a reaction in the hearts of all who heard. Many praised her brave decision to do the unimaginable and forgive someone who had taken so very much from her, who had acted with such hate toward her. But many still didn't understand why she had forgiven someone who did not deserve it, seeing her choice as insane and even wrong.[3]

The Christian nihilist philosopher Søren Kierkegaard once said that "when love forgives, the miracle of faith occurs."[4] Forgiveness is something we all can agree, in theory, is a right and good thing, especially when given to us. But in practice, especially when we are asked to forgive, it can seem almost impossible. Forgiveness goes against every natural instinct we have. Even children struggle with the concept of forgiveness when wronged, offering a begrudging "I forgive you, I guess," and only upon being made to. Forgiveness is counterintuitive to our brains and feels almost painful to offer—especially when we've been sinned against in a way that has caused us significant loss. Which is why it's one of the most difficult and countercultural things Jesus ever asked us—his followers—to do and keep doing to everyone, for everything, always.

In the gospel of Matthew, Peter, Jesus's disciple, asked whether he only needed to forgive someone seven times, to which Jesus replied, "I tell you, not seven times, but seventy-seven times" (18:22). This response no doubt caused Peter's heart to drop because he knew that Jesus wasn't giving a number for how many times are required but was telling Peter to forgive endlessly. And this is a nice idea for all of us in theory, but in practice it becomes almost insurmountable for some offenses.

Forgiveness is one of the most difficult and countercultural things Jesus ever asked us to do and keep doing to everyone, for everything, always.

We live in a world where wrongs are committed daily against society as a whole and against us personally. Sometimes these wrongs are committed in a public and far-off way, in the form of a celebrity tweeting something insensitive and hurtful about us or our community, or a politician carelessly signing legislation that brings about real destruction in our lives. But more often and more intensely felt, we are hurt by those close to us, whose actions have a large, long-lasting, and detrimental effect on our lives. We all know the sting of a lover saying something hurtful or lying to us, a parent mistreating or criticizing us, or a trusted friend betraying us. And when this happens, it suddenly feels like the world we long to be right is now wrong.

Most of us, deep down, have an intrinsic belief that there is a balance in the world, and when someone commits a sin against us, that balance is thrown off, and the rightness of our world is suddenly out of whack. The wholeness we desire to exist in has been fractured. And when faced with this fracture, the proposition of forgiving feels like an action that simply ignores the real imbalance that now exists in the world and our own lives.

The idea of cancel culture—both public and personal—partly comes out of a desire to right the world of the wrongs we and others have felt. For balance to happen, we believe there must be a punitive action for the perpetrator equal to the wrong committed. This is not a wrong desire—this is actually a desire from God (Ecclesiastes 3:17). God created the world to be a whole and beautiful place of order and balance, and throughout Scripture we see God involve himself in the ongoing work of pulling the world back to wholeness from the bad people who seem to continue to break it. And this God-designed work is good, necessary, and godly—it stops hateful people from continuing their destructive acts and it rights their wrongs. This is the concept we know of as *justice*—a word the *Britannica Dictionary* defines as "the process or result of using laws to fairly judge and punish crimes and criminals."[5] Justice is a good thing and something not only to value but to carry out, as commanded by God (Jeremiah 22:3 and Micah 6:8).

The problem of forgiveness doesn't arise from or conflict with exacting justice, but the problem arises *after* justice has been served. It was right and good for the Charleston shooter to be arrested, stand trial, and be sentenced for his acts. But even when he had been put in chains and faced the death penalty, the residual hurt and anger that resulted from his actions remained both in the world and in the hearts of the victims' families. Which was why their choice to forgive was so supernaturally shocking.

Often today and throughout history, humans find that after justice has been served, boundaries are drawn in either societal or personal ways, and wrongs have been made right. Yet the heavy, residual emotions of hate, anger, and disdain can persist past the justice that was exacted. In this modern age, we conflate the idea of *justice* with that of *revenge*, which the *Britannica Dictionary* defines as "the act of doing something to hurt someone because that person did something that hurt you."[6] Revenge is a natural human desire to not only bring an end to destruction and make it right but to exact the same amount (or more) of the hurt we experience back upon those who hurt us, even past the point where justice has been served. With this confusion about justice and revenge, we too often cite justice as a reason to slake our lust for vengeance, a practice that has created a world of angry and vindictive people.

There's a ubiquitous saying often attributed to the peaceful revolutionary Gandhi, who famously fought violent oppression with a philosophy of nonviolence. It goes, "An eye for an eye leaves the whole world blind." And we currently live in a world where we have become blind with anger, rage, and disdain as we act out our vengeance upon those who have hurt us. The words for this quote originally came from Jesus, who addressed a people who were dealing with the same issue two thousand years ago.

> You have heard that it was said, "Eye for eye, and tooth for tooth." But I tell you, do not resist an evil person. If anyone slaps you on the right cheek, turn to them the other cheek also. And if anyone wants to sue you and take your shirt, hand over your coat as well. If anyone forces you to go one mile, go with them two miles. Give to the one who asks you, and do not turn away from the one who wants to borrow from you.
>
> You have heard that it was said, "Love your neighbor and hate your enemy." But I tell you, love your enemies and pray for those who persecute you. (Matthew 5:38–44)

These beautiful words have rung throughout an angry and vengeful history of violence and death, drawing those who are brave enough to listen back to the way of healing and wholeness. But to many they are just words. Words that seem almost absurd in the face of the constant injustices and destructive actions committed against us on a daily basis. Jesus cared about and exacted justice, but he also knew the human proclivity to seek vengeance instead of justice. He knew that this temptation we all face would, as the quote said, "leave the whole world blind." It's easy to read the words of Jesus and agree in the abstract with these ideas of forgiveness and grace. But it's so much harder in flesh-and-blood, real-life situations where residual anger and rage linger so that, even after justice has been served, it can feel impossible to forgive or see why we should in the first place.

So why should we, and how do we?

Forgiveness in Action

There's a lyric to one of my favorite songs, "Middle of June," by Noah Gundersen, that says hatred is like a sharp knife that cuts with no pain. In this particular piece of poetry, Noah's words get straight to the matter of why we should forgive—primarily because it's freeing and healing for us (Colossians 3:13–15; Mark 11:25). Refusing to forgive or holding on to the desire for revenge, especially beyond the moment of justice, doesn't accomplish the wholeness we desire in the world or in our hearts. Instead it simply extends the fracture with every passing year. We hold the knife by the blade, as Noah's song says, squeezing tighter and tighter, but the only thing unforgiveness accomplishes is our bleeding out anger and bitterness that will ultimately bring about the destruction of ourselves. We know this intellectually, and there are countless movies about the demise of a character so bent on revenge that it consumes all the good in their life and ultimately kills them. But when it comes to our own personal lives, we seem to forget these moral tales and opt for wrapping the fingers of our hearts and minds around a hot stone of hurt that weighs us down and steals our joy. We believe that vengeance, which is ultimately just unforgiveness acted out, will bring us the catharsis we so desire. But it's a lie—it never does.

There's an old saying that brings this point home: "Unforgiveness is like drinking poison and expecting someone else to die." This pithy phrase is actually backed by science. Studies have shown that people who refuse to forgive and who foster deep grudges are far more likely to experience severe depression and post-traumatic stress disorder, as well as multiple physical health conditions.[7] In her article "The Power of Forgiveness: Why Revenge Doesn't Work," author and psychiatrist Judith Orloff says,

> Forgiveness is a paradigm-shifting solution for transforming anger. It liberates you from the trap of endless revenge so that you can experience more joy and connection. Forgiveness does more for you than anyone else because it liberates you from negativity and lets you move forward.[8]

Moving forward—growing and evolving—is necessary for any living organism to exist. If something isn't growing, then it's decaying and dying. And when we don't forgive, we hold ourselves back from life. Psychology has discovered what Jesus has been saying for two thousand years—forgiveness is the only path to wholeness. It's not just something we offer for someone else's sake, but for our own. The longer we hold on to the blade of vengeance and unforgiveness, the longer we allow the cut in our soul to bleed. But the sooner we take the brave step to forgive and let go, the sooner we will taste freedom and experience the wholeness we long for.

But the *why* of anything is always easier than the *how*. We can understand something intellectually and even agree with it. But the *how*—putting it into action—is almost always more difficult.

One of the most powerful scenes the world has ever known is the image of Jesus hanging on a cross—an innocent man, in the midst of being brutally murdered by a screaming mob—and uttering these world-shattering words: "Father, forgive them, for they know not what they do" (Luke 23:34 ESV).

Here we have the Son of God being killed by the ones he formed, created, and loved. And though he has every right to look out with anger, to use his power to exact justified revenge, he doesn't. Jesus chooses to forgive, and in doing so redeems the entire world. But it wasn't just that mob he was looking at who needed forgiveness—it was all of us. We are all that mob whom Jesus willingly died for and offered unearned forgiveness to. Yes, you and me. We are in need of forgiveness. And this realization that we have sinned, hurt people, made mistakes, and caused fractures in the world can change everything.

As we go about trying to forgive those who have done the unforgivable in our lives, recognizing that we are also in need of forgiveness has the power to change our perspectives so we are able to offer the mercy we've been given.

Forgiveness = Freedom

Years back I found myself in a familiar scene to the one I detailed in the opening of this chapter, but with the roles reversed. I was the one who was pleading for forgiveness from a loved one I had wronged in a heavy and real way. I recognized the look of frustration, hurt, and pain in their eyes because it was the same look I had assuredly had on my face when I was the one who needed to forgive. My heart sank, and I let my gaze fall to the floor. I didn't deserve mercy. I knew that my own selfishness and thoughtlessness had caused real and lasting pain. I waited in the silence, the words of my apology still hanging between us. Then I felt a hand on my shoulder. I looked up. There were tears in my loved one's eyes as they said the words I so longed to hear, the words that would set me free.

"I forgive you."

Forgiveness is a universally agreed-upon good, something we all know is of high benefit, and the effects of not giving it are devastating—to the people who have hurt us and to ourselves. But actually making the choice to forgive, not just once but over and over again, can feel impossible. The action of acknowledging our own need for grace and mercy can change our entire psyche and souls, bringing us to a place where we are able to offer forgiveness to others. But accepting our own sin, faults, and failures is an entirely separate issue in and of itself.

> Then Peter came to Jesus and asked, "Lord, how many times shall I forgive my brother or sister who sins against me? Up to seven times?"
>
> Jesus answered, "I tell you, not seven times, but seventy-seven times.
>
> "Therefore, the kingdom of heaven is like a king who wanted to settle accounts with his servants. As he began the settlement, a man who owed him ten thousand bags of gold was brought to him. Since he was not able to pay, the master ordered that he and his wife and his children and all that he had be sold to repay the debt.
>
> "At this the servant fell on his knees before him. 'Be patient with me,' he begged, 'and I will pay back everything.' The servant's master took pity on him, canceled the debt and let him go.
>
> "But when that servant went out, he found one of his fellow servants who owed him a hundred silver coins. He grabbed him and began to choke him. 'Pay back what you owe me!' he demanded.
>
> "His fellow servant fell to his knees and begged him, 'Be patient with me, and I will pay it back.'
>
> "But he refused. Instead, he went off and had the man thrown into prison until he could pay the debt. When the other servants saw what had happened, they were outraged and went and told their master everything that had happened.
>
> "Then the master called the servant in. 'You wicked servant,' he said, 'I canceled all that debt of yours because you

begged me to. Shouldn't you have had mercy on your fellow servant just as I had on you?' In anger his master handed him over to the jailers to be tortured, until he should pay back all he owed.

"This is how my heavenly Father will treat each of you unless you forgive your brother or sister from your heart." (Matthew 18:21–35)

Chapter 7

CANCELING GOD

The problem of reconciling human suffering with the existence of a God who loves, is only insoluble so long as we attach a trivial meaning to the word "love," and look on things as if man were the centre of them. Man is not the centre. God does not exist for the sake of man. Man does not exist for his own sake. "Thou hast created all things, and for thy pleasure they are and were created." We were made not primarily that we may love God (though we were made for that too) but that God may love us, that we may become objects in which the divine love may rest "well pleased."

—C. S. Lewis, *The Problem of Pain*

I stepped off the mat and into the shower for the fifth time that day. My six-foot-three, 240-pound hulking body strained the old, cracked tub in my small apartment bathroom as I tried to fit behind the cheap plastic curtain I threw shut behind me. A wave of frustration and anger bubbled up inside me as I turned the faucets that brought the scalding water pouring over my tired body. As I picked up the soap, I hoped and prayed that this time the cleansing ritual would make me feel clean. But prayer had never helped before. I wanted it to. I longed for even a moment of relief from the mental illness the psychiatrists had diagnosed me with almost two decades ago, called obsessive-compulsive disorder, or OCD. But no matter how much I had petitioned God, the barrage of unwanted thoughts hadn't let up, for even a moment, in my thirty-plus years.

When I was younger, desperate for some kind of relief, I had allowed a pastor to lay hands on and pray over me during a worship service in youth group after he promised God would do a miracle. But when I woke up the next morning with all the usual compulsions and uncontrollable thoughts, I didn't understand why God hadn't done something. I had truly believed and had faith he'd fix me. I did and felt the things I was supposed to. And nothing . . .

In the decade and a half since that prayer, I had gotten used to the idea that I had a lifelong mental illness. What I hadn't gotten used to was why God allowed me to be born with it and why he refused to do anything about it.

The same frustration with the Divine that I felt all those years ago still plagued my mind as I stepped out of the shower yet again, hoping I could feel clean long enough to work on passion projects before the inevitable and unwanted thoughts descended. I had woken up with a plan to work on the things I loved—to write my book, to be productive, and to have a good day. But by late afternoon, I realized I had now wasted most of my day performing obsessive compulsions. Defeated, I collapsed on my bed, too tired and too depressed to do any of the things that brought my soul joy.

My wife looked on sympathetically, now used to the nonstop showers, repeated hand washing, and endless cleaning rituals. She served as a witness to my struggle. I buried my head in my pillow and let out a muffled cry of frustration and anger at God, at his inability or, even worse, his unwillingness to help me in the midst of my pain.

It's God's Fault (Not)

There's a scene in the '90s movie *The Apostle*, written, directed, and starred in by the great Robert Duvall, where a pastor who has spent his life trying to follow, honor, and serve God is faced with an unthinkable series of events—including betrayal, infidelity, and murder—that destroy his life. Toward the end of the movie, the pastor confronts God, and in a whirlwind of angry confusion, he yells at the Almighty, blaming him for the painful fate that has befallen him.

"I'm confused. I'm mad. I love you, Lord. I love you. But I'm mad at you. I am mad at *you*!"[1] the pastor shouts, pointing his fingers toward heaven with an honest and rage-filled accusation, before waiting for a reply that does not come.

This movie released in 1997 and went on to find critical acclaim, and even an Oscar nomination, as a result of its honesty about a reality that almost every human will face in their lifetime—the inclination to blame God . . . and even to cancel him.

Blaming and canceling God isn't a new idea—in fact, it's as old as history itself. A similar story written over 2,500 years ago and found in ancient Scriptures is the epic and tragic tale of Job—which begins in storybook-like fashion with "In the land of Uz there lived a man whose name was Job. This man was blameless and upright; he feared God and shunned evil" (Job 1:1). This story details a narrative about the blameless man Job. Terrible and devastating fates befall him after Satan sets out to prove to God that his most faithful follower will curse his name if enough bad things happen to him. But even after disease, devastation, and the deaths of his children, Job refuses to curse God and instead praises him, proving the devil wrong. It's an epic story full of flowing poetry, beautiful prose, and deep theological insights. But it's also one that has left many a reader scratching their head, as many of us, especially today, cannot see the logic of not blaming God for the devastation that takes place in our lives when it seems so apparent that ultimately the fault for the condition of the world lays in God's hands.

Is God to Blame?

In what I consider to be the best film I've written and directed, *Don't Know Jack*, we follow the story of a troubled young man named Jack, who, upon deciding to end his own life, gives a therapist, Leslie, one hour to convince him not to. Throughout the hour-long conversation, Leslie probes Jack to see what has happened in his life to cause him to take such drastic action. They talk through Jack's story, brought to life in flashbacks that detail his life, love, family, and trauma, all in hopes of identifying the root of Jack's frustration and despair. But after the usual psychological trails lead nowhere, eventually their conversation turns to God, and it's there Leslie discovers Jack's deep anger toward God for the pain and loss he's experienced. After discussing apologetics and theology, Leslie asks the question that prompts the following exchange:

> **Leslie:** Do *you* believe in God?
>
> **Jack:** I wanted to. For so long. I mean, what kid—or person, for that matter—wouldn't want to believe that someone cared enough to make us exist? Who wouldn't want to believe that we actually matter and there's more than this when we die?
>
> **Leslie:** But you don't.
>
> **Jack:** No.
>
> **Leslie:** Why not?
>
> **Jack:** I'd rather not believe in God than hate him. 'Cause if he is real, then he's a bastard who says he loves us while laughing as he watches us stumbling around down here in the dark. If God exists, I'd have to hate him. And a life spent hating someone you can't change or convince to care about you is a waste.
>
> **Leslie:** Like your dad?
>
> **Jack:** Sure, just like my dad.

Leslie: What if he does care about you?

Jack: My dad?

Leslie: God.

Jack: He couldn't.

Leslie: Why not?

Jack: Because he lets bad things happen.

Leslie: Maybe he can't intervene.

Jack: Then he's not God.

Leslie: I guess that's one way to see it.

Jack: How could any dad who loved his kid watch them get run over, get hooked on drugs, get raped, or kill themselves—without intervening?

Leslie: That's the age-old question.

Jack: Exactly . . .

Leslie: What do you mean by that?

Jack: I mean, if it's a question that after all these years people are still asking, it means we still haven't been given an answer good enough to stop asking it.

Leslie: Just because we can't prove something doesn't mean it's not real. If there's nothing in your life that's bigger than all this, then you're doomed to a hopeless existence.[2]

I won't tell you the end of the film. But Jack's struggle to believe in God's goodness and Jack's desire, in essence, to cancel God are two concerns that many of us, including myself, have experienced in the midst of our tragic stories.

The Problem of Evil

When we are no longer able to blame people, either personal or collective, we are left with what feels like the only available option: to blame God for the hurt, pain, and unexplained devastation we witness and experience. Once we blame him, placing the responsibility for the bad in the world at his feet, we then proceed to ultimately cancel him—we banish him from our lives and culture as a whole, utilizing the same methodology of cancellation we employ for disgraced celebrities and fallen figures. And it makes sense. God and his followers constantly tell us how great he is, describing him as "all powerful" and "all loving." Many of us sincerely believed the claims about God we heard or grew up with, just to have our sincerity blow up in our faces when the darkness of life falls and it seems God and his love are nowhere to be found. This causes us to feel like fools for having trusted in something that ultimately seems to have been a lie. So if God is real, why doesn't he intervene, either in our personal problems (like divorce, financial ruin, sickness, accidents, death, and abuse) or in the universal ones that affect the world (like war, poverty, natural disasters, and disease)?

Many of us sincerely believed the claims about God we heard or grew up with, just to have our sincerity blow up in our faces when the darkness of life falls.

In a matter of a few years, we've seen wildfires and tsunamis tear through and destroy the homes, lands, and lives of good people. Wars and genocides that rip nations apart while killing countless civilians. Acts of terrorism that maim and murder innocent lives. Economic ruin that leaves families hungry and desperate. Unchecked corruption that oppresses the most defenseless of us all. And even a pandemic plague that brought death to millions in a startlingly short time. During all this, it seemed to many that if there was a God, or at least if God was "good" like he says he is, he'd have done something about it. He'd have stopped it.

But we were left to look on in horror in the midst of deafening heavenly silence. It makes sense that if we can't blame others for the atrocities we experience, surely we can blame an all-powerful God who seems either unable or unwilling to do something about the suffering of the world he claims to love.

When asked what he would say to God if he found out that he is real and had an opportunity to meet him, beloved actor, comedian, and outspoken atheist Stephen Fry had this to say:

> I'd say, bone cancer in children? What's that about? How dare you? How dare you create a world to which there is such misery that is not our fault? It's not right. It's utterly, utterly evil. Why should I respect a capricious, mean-minded, stupid God who creates a world that is so full of injustice and pain? That's what I would say.[3]

Stephen's remarks, while blunt and offensive to some, strike at the heart of why so many of us find ourselves blaming God. If God is unable to stop the bad in the world from happening, he is not powerful. But even worse, if he is powerful enough and doesn't, how could he possibly be good?

In his book *God Is Not Great*, the late British writer, philosopher, and skeptic Christopher Hitchens wrote about God's elusiveness when it comes to the devastation in the world, quoting Epicurus's ancient questions: "Is [God] willing to prevent evil but not able? Then is he impotent. Is he able but not willing? Then is he malevolent. Is he both able and willing? Whence then is evil?"[4]

Epicurus's words serve as a succinct cry of a modern culture that has, in large part, in one form or another, canceled God.

In the past twenty years, since the turn of the century, church membership and religious affiliation has been steadily declining. According to Gallup research from 2020, only 47 percent of Americans regularly attended a religious service, which is down twenty points since 2000.[5] Similarly, according to Pew Research, in 1990, 90 percent of Americans identified as Christians, but in just a few decades, that percentage has dropped to 63 percent.[6] Now many Americans fall under the category of "religious nones," a term that has arisen to describe those who are atheist, agnostic, or nothing in particular, and this statistic continues to grow every year. If we look specifically at younger people, the statistics become even more alarming. According to Barna Research, about 64 percent of youths walk away from church after graduating high school.[7]

Even aside from the statistics, anecdotally we see the phenomenon of people, particularly young people, leaving God behind. We watch as people we have known and loved struggle with their faith and ultimately give it up. Which leaves us wondering what went wrong. In the past ten years, the term *deconstruction* has been popularized by notable Christian pastors, worship leaders, and authors who, for a myriad of reasons, walk away from their faith after questioning their beliefs and finding themselves unable to reconcile what they've been told about God and what they've experienced. The deconstruction movement has sparked fear in the hearts of church leaders and Christian thinkers, who have labeled it an "epidemic."[8]

In response to this uncomfortable reality, Christians have tried many things to retain and attract people to stay within the confines of Christianity's walls. We've tried being more culturally relevant by playing modern music, dressing pastors in hip styles, and utilizing slick video presentations during our services. We've tried holding debates where we argue our side in an attempt to show the rationality of our beliefs over others'. But in large part, we've mostly shamed and ignored the questions of the ones threatening to walk away. It's easy as Christians to want to dismiss and condemn this slow exodus—this cancellation of God. But we know that dismissing or shaming someone over an experience never brings relational redemption. Perhaps, rather than reactively shaming people struggling with and losing their faith, we would be better served in understanding why they feel the urge to walk away from something we believe is the ultimate fulfillment of truth, beauty, and purpose.

So why are we seeing so many choosing to walk away from and cancel God? There are a thousand reasons, but one of the central and most potent reasons is found in what theologians and apologetic philosophers call "the problem of evil," which can be summed up as the problem of reconciling the existence of evil with the supposed omnipotence and perfect goodness of God.[9] This has likely been a burning question in the hearts of people since first formally posed by the ancient Greek philosopher Epicurus.[10]

A survey by Barna Group, commissioned by apologist, bestselling author, and journalist Lee Strobel, asked respondents, "If you could ask God one question and knew he would give you an answer, what would you ask?" The most common response was, "Why is there so much pain and suffering?"[11] This leads me to believe that one of the biggest reasons people leave God has less to do with there not being enough skinny jeans, worship anthems, or even solid arguments present in our faith, but rather a real and unanswered question that digs into the hearts and minds of former and potential Jesus followers: How could this loving God allow all this brokenness, pain, and hurt both in my life and in the world around me? Much like the pastor in the movie *The Apostle*, many of us struggle to reconcile the pain we experience in our lives with a so-called loving God, so we go about ridding ourselves of needing or depending on something we have learned will disappoint us. So the question becomes, if we're honest, why *shouldn't* we cancel God?

Many theologians, philosophers, and pastors have grappled with this question, trying to make sense of God's apparent absence in our hurt. Some posit that all the evil is ordained and orchestrated by God as a means to accomplish his will. But such a position may make it difficult to call God "good" if the evil in the world is his own invention and direction, and it may affirm the accusations that God is actually evil. Others explain it as God allowing evil if we don't pray or believe hard enough, and he intercedes when we achieve a certain emotional state or prove our dedication through religious displays, or sometimes just randomly when he decides to. Which may not reflect the God of infinite grace and love we see in Scripture, as it's hard to believe in God's goodness and power if it's entirely dependent on our actions. This may portray God as petty and unpredictable.

And while these two have largely been the explanations given to this seemingly unanswerable question, maybe there's another answer that might get to the heart of what's going on and help us understand just how perfectly good God is, why there's evil in the world, and why instead of canceling God, we should run to him.

Free to Choose

My friend Zak Schmoll is a prolific author, respected professor, and accomplished academic of theology and philosophy. I met Zak when he came on my podcast, *The Overthinkers*, for the episode "If God Is Real, Why Does Evil Exist?" Zak spoke on the subject of the problem of evil, as he has spent decades studying, grappling with, and searching to understand this question that seems so relevant to the hearts and minds of today. But unlike many academics who study subjects that don't directly affect them in their remote and safe environment, Zak is especially equipped to speak on this difficult question because he was born with a degenerative spinal disease that has left him needing a wheelchair for mobility, with limited movement and the need for constant care. To most of us who will never face this kind of deep and lasting struggle, this is an unthinkable and devastatingly painful reality to imagine. One that would make anger at or disbelief in God seem justified. But Zak does believe in and love God, so much, in fact, that he's dedicated his life to helping others know and love him too. But why?

In his book *Disability and the Problem of Evil*, which details Zak's story of struggle and his reasons for believing that God is still good and worthy of love, he lays out a compelling case that looks to Scripture, reason, and emotion. He focuses on free will being both a gift from a loving God and the cause of evil in the world. Free will is something we were each endowed with from our Creator. It's what differentiates us from every other living being. We are not bound to mere instinct, like animals, or left to the chaos of nature, like cells and plants. Instead we have minds that can make choices and decide the actions we take.

The ancient Latin phrase *imago Dei* means "image of God" and is based on the scriptural truth that we were created in the very *image* of God, and in his likeness, he has given us a will.[12] This is a wonderful thing, for as a result of free will, we are able to choose to be a part of the beauty he created, to be in relationship with both him and the ones around us. True love only exists out of choice. My wife and I share a true and real love because we chose each other. There was and is no coercion or force. We made an act of will toward each other. But free will can also be a terrible thing, as we are as free to make destructive choices out of selfish ambition, insecurity, and anger—choices that have the ability to cause great hurt to both ourselves and others. Our free will enables us to be in an authentically true relationship with God, but it also enables us to walk away from him if we choose.

God Cares

In Genesis we see that God—after creating the world, universe, and reality itself—sits back and, while gazing at his creation, declares it "good" (1:31). But not just good in the "nice" sense, like we would say about a good meal, but good in the fullest sense—where his creation is complete, whole, and working. Like a machine that runs perfectly and is aesthetically pleasing. God is both an artist and engineer who designed the entire world in a way that displays his order and beauty. Then as the story continues, he designs us—the human, Adam and Eve—with the same order and beauty. But unlike the rest of creation, he creates us in his own image with our own wills, bearing his own powerful and consequential ability to choose. And we know what happens shortly after. Endowed with the God-given power to make choices, Adam and Eve use their wills to reject the opportunity to live in harmony with God's creation and in relationship with their Creator. In their own hubris, they choose to rebel in a way that fractures the order and beauty God had created for them and all of creation to live in. This breaks God's heart, but he allows their choice, as his greatest desire is for his creations to choose to be with him, and the only way that choice is possible is by giving them the ability to choose not to be with him.[13]

The story of Adam and Eve is not just history but also represents Jesus's preference for metaphorical parables, which each of us can see ourselves in. I think the story of Adam and Eve represents the choice that lies before us every day, every moment: to choose to live in relationship with God and in harmony with his creation, or to, in our own hubris, go our own way against the design God created for us, thus fracturing ourselves and our relationships with God and the entire world.

We need not look far, or even outside of ourselves, to see the proclivity every human has—being made in the image of God—to try to play God and use our free will to make choices that break the beauty and design God has created. We each eat that apple every day. We each add our own personal crack to the fracture that's been growing throughout all human history and has now spread to every inch of the world. Of course it makes sense to want to blame and cancel God for the pain and despair in the world, but the uncomfortable truth is that if we look close enough, we will find that fracture is man-made.

God's heart breaks for the sadness and pain in the world (Psalm 34:18), but he also respects our wills, as it is the only way to have a true and loving relationship with him (Deuteronomy 30:15–20).

But he didn't just leave us alone in the pieces of the world we broke, standing off in smug indifference; instead he cares. He cares so much that he came to us and gave his life to conquer that fracture we have made, so that the world could be made right. So that we could be made right. He offers us this relationship even now, even after all these thousands of years of us humans rebelling and going our own way, destroying the world around us. He invites us into a relationship with him, one that will redeem the world and return it to what it was supposed to be and return us to who we were created to be. In the last book of the Bible, Revelation, which echoes the first book, Genesis, God's spirit writes this to us:

> He will wipe away every tear from their eyes, and death shall be no more, neither shall there be mourning, nor crying, nor pain anymore, for the former things have passed away. (Revelation 21:4 ESV)

God is not to blame for our hurt and pain. And when it comes to who we ought to cancel for the destruction in the world, depressingly the rightful owners of that sentence are us, all of us—Democrat and Republican, atheist and believer, man and woman, Black, Brown, and White, all of us. Admitting our guilt is the first step toward experiencing the redemption he promises, so why do so few do it? And why is it so hard?

> My God, my God, why have you abandoned me?
> Why are you so far away when I groan for help?
> Every day I call to you, my God, but you do not answer.
> Every night I lift my voice, but I find no relief.
> (Psalm 22:1–2 NLT)

Chapter 8

WHAT HAVE I DONE?

The fault, dear Brutus, is not in our stars, but in ourselves, that we are underlings.
—WILLIAM SHAKESPEARE, *JULIUS CAESAR*

I had found myself at the end of a whirlwind year and a half of heartbreak and loss. Fresh off a devastating divorce, I had left LA and moved to New York City in hopes of leaving the ghosts behind and starting a new life. I had hoped that if I ran fast enough from one city to another, I could outrun my own brokenness, which seemed to be following me like a shadow, nipping at my heels and looming over my head.

I tried to start a new life in a new city and a new apartment. I had rented a room in a basement with no windows. When I would tell people where I was living, they would say that they could never live in a place with no light, but I liked it. It felt safe, no light shining into the shelter of darkness I lived in. I tried my best to be "okay," to do things that normal people do, pretend the past didn't exist, and move forward. But little by little I distanced myself from the world. I spent more and more time inside, sometimes not leaving for days at a time, just sitting on my bed, watching old TV shows, eating comfort food (instead of feeling). I would venture out sometimes for exercise and fresh air, but the light hurt my eyes, the people triggered my severe OCD, and the walking wore me out. I went on like this for months, until the landlord informed me I had to vacate, as the upstairs apartment wanted to expand to make my room a part of their home.

Suddenly I had to face the idea of leaving the shadows where I had been hiding all my hurt, dysfunction, and fears, and step into the light. One night after I had packed my things into one lonely box, I undressed to take a shower and suddenly caught my reflection in the mirror that I so often tried to avoid, and there staring back at me was someone I didn't recognize. The man in the mirror was fifty pounds heavier than when he had moved in and had a sunken and sad face, and in his eyes lay the rubble of a broken person. As I confronted this reflection of what I had become, my mind whispered, *What have I done?* It was there in that moment that I was given a choice—ignore the destruction my choices had led me to or finally look at and reckon with the mess I had made.

Confronting Ourselves

There's a classic book by a now-canceled nineteenth-century author entitled *The Picture of Dorian Gray*, written by the once-beloved Oscar Wilde. The story revolves around Dorian, who, being young, handsome, and rich, has a portrait painted of himself, which he hangs in his house. As the story unfolds, Dorian walks down a dark road of selfishness, anger, and pride, secretly committing cruel and heartless acts against the world and the ones around him. While Dorian appears to become even more beautiful and youthful to any who might gaze upon him, the portrait hanging in his house reveals the reality of who he really is. The portrait begins, bit by bit, to display the wretchedness that lies within his soul.

Dorian takes little notice of the changing portrait reflecting his inner reality, until one day he can no longer ignore the perverse ugliness his actions have resulted in. Dorian is suddenly faced with the reality of what he's done and who he has become. He didn't see the creeping fracture that had been crawling over his heart until the painting finally revealed the grotesque and broken results of Dorian's decisions.

It is here Dorian is faced with a choice. He can recognize the destruction that has taken place from his own heartless decisions, deal with the consequences, and make the choice to change. Or he can hide the portrait in the darkness of his attic, where no one will have the chance to discover who he really is. Dorian chooses the latter, unable to face the reality of what he's done and who he's become.

The "What have I done?" moment is a famous concept we see throughout the greatest literature, films, and plays. It's an emotional scene that usually takes place toward the end of a story, where the protagonist, or sometimes the antagonist, is suddenly confronted with the ramifications of what they've done and, more importantly, who they've become and what they really are. Up until then, they've been blind to the destruction they are causing, often justifying their actions with twisted morality or perverse reason. We read this concept in great books like *The Strange Case of Dr. Jekyll and Mr. Hyde*, as Dr. Jekyll takes his own life after finding himself trapped by his violent ways in search of power. We watch it in films like *Titanic*, where Thomas Andrews, the designer of the great ship, faces his own hubris in foolishly believing the *Titanic* to be unsinkable. We experience it in plays like *All My Sons*, where Joe Keller is faced with the fact that his dishonesty killed his own son. We even see it in Scripture, when Judas realizes he has betrayed his Savior for a few pieces of silver and hangs himself, unable to live with the guilt.

It's no accident that this moment, this concept, appears in so many stories we have told for all of human history. The reason it persists is because the "What have I done?" moment is a universal human experience, one we can all understand and connect to in a real and emotional way. Which one of us hasn't felt the bitter sting of facing the depressing and dire consequences of our own mistakes?

There have been a handful of times in my life when I've had to finally stop and look at the destruction I've caused either to my own life or to others'. It hurts, sometimes almost unbearably so. But it's here in this moment, as we are confronted with who we are and what we've done, that we have a choice. We can turn our gaze, run and hide, and ignore the difficult and uncomfortable reality that we are not who we should be and have acted in ways that have brought fracture to ourselves and others. Or we can bravely face our own brokenness.

Mea Culpa

Throughout New York City there are countless beautiful and historic Catholic churches, sitting as beacons of light among the endless apartment buildings and skyscrapers. I will sometimes attend a Mass with my friend to experience a faith tradition different from the one I grew up with. I love the reverence, order, and form of the liturgical service that takes place inside the echoing walls covered with stained-glass windows, among statues of saints, and beneath towering ceilings of intricately carved arches. I love the Scripture readings, the reciting of creeds, and the wise homilies. But there's one part of the service that always affects my heart and stays in my mind long after the final blessing is given: the Confiteor, during which the congregation stands together and in unison recites these words:

> I confess to almighty God, and to you, my brothers and sisters, that I have greatly sinned through my thoughts and in my words, in what I have done, and in what I have failed to do, through my fault, through my fault, through my most grievous fault.

For each of the three *fault* statements, we beat our breasts with our fists as a physical picture of our sorrow and acknowledgment of our faults, our most grievous faults.

This is a powerful moment, as it's one of the only places in modern culture where I have ever seen people gather together and recognize their own brokenness, much less in such a public display. And it's not just a once-in-a-while Christmas and Easter thing. This act of penitence takes place at every Mass, and it means this: To be a part of this faith community, you must regularly acknowledge and confess your brokenness. Something the rest of the world seems wholly uninterested in or unable to do.

The Confiteor was originally spoken in Latin and uses the phrase *mea culpa*, which means "my fault."[1] But this phrase, this idea, is so powerful—and perhaps so needed (and underused) in our modern world—that it has been adopted into the English dictionary. *Collins Dictionary* defines *mea culpa* as "an acknowledgment of one's responsibility."[2] The liturgical church does this every week at every service, because they know that humans have a remarkable ability to forget, ignore, and hide from their faults. We do this in a myriad of ways, one of our favorites being to point out the faults of others (canceling people) to overlook our own. Like Adam in the garden, we sometimes justify our behavior as good and righteous, or at least understandable—that is, not that bad. And sometimes we just ignore it altogether, distracting ourselves with the many engrossing activities modernity offers.

We live in a culture seemingly dedicated to helping us avoid, ignore, or escape our own "What have I done?" moments, a culture that keeps us away from ever having to say "mea culpa" and beat our breasts at the realization of the terrible things we've done and the broken people we've become. Popular slogans like "you're perfect the way you are," books with titles like *I'm Okay—You're Okay*, movements that teach us how to find the specks in others' eyes while ignoring the logs in our own, and an endless supply of podcasts, speakers, and public intellectuals assure us that our problems are someone else's fault. Culture does everything it can to keep you from facing your mess because there's money to be made, loyalty to be bought, and followers to be gained by assuring you that there's nothing wrong with you, something we all deeply wish were true. But it's a lie. However, it's one we eat up to avoid the pain that comes from looking at ourselves with honest introspection.

Many of us will spend our entire lives believing these lies and employing these tactics to avoid and run from our own "What have I done?" moments. But with every averted gaze and escape route taken, our brokenness isn't fixed, and the fracture of our hearts, minds, and souls spreads.

Look in the Mirror

The apostle Paul, who wrote the majority of the New Testament, had his own rather dramatic "What have I done?" moment. Before he was a Scripture writer, theologian, and world-traveling evangelist, he persecuted, imprisoned, and even approved the murders of the very people he would one day lead (Acts 8:1–3).

After the death and resurrection of Jesus, the Messiah appeared to Paul—known also as Saul—in a flash of light on a dusty road toward the Syrian town of Damascus, confronting him: "Saul, Saul, why do you persecute me?" (9:4). This was the moment the great apostle and saint faced the reality of what he had done and who he was. Paul's life changed on that road after being forced to confront the mess he'd made of his life. Paul went on to become the greatest theologian and evangelist the world has ever seen, but even as he reached worldwide respect and honor as a man of God, Paul never stopped the practice of acknowledging and confronting the broken parts of himself, even beginning one of his more influential writings by calling himself the "worst" of sinners (1 Timothy 1:15).

Most of us won't have a "What have I done?" scene in which God appears to us in a flash of light, but all of us, no matter how hard we try to avoid or run from it, will find ourselves having to face what we've done and who we are. Mine was a look into a literal mirror that night, where I was confronted with a person looking back whom I didn't recognize. Your moment will happen too (if it hasn't already)—the moment you'll find yourself looking at your own "mirror," reflecting the hard truth of your broken humanity. And this moment hurts—it hurts like hell. Because gazing upon our brokenness reminds us just how far we are from who we should be, who we were created to be. But it's in that moment when we have one of the most important choices we can ever make—to look and realize or to turn away and keep running.

In the New Testament, James talked about God's Word being the catalyst to showing us our need and the reality of our faults. He said that it acts like a mirror that can reveal the truth of who we really are, but we have to actually look, without averting our gaze, even when it hurts. If we don't, he said, "It is like glancing at your face in a mirror. You see yourself, walk away, and forget what you look like" (James 1:23–24 NLT). Most of us want to forget what we look like; it's uncomfortable and even painful to face our ugliness. Most of us, like Dorian, want to keep that image of ourselves hidden deep in the dark where no one, especially ourselves, can see it.

It's one of the most important choices we can ever make—to look and realize or to turn away and keep running.

But why is it so very hard to be honest with ourselves about ourselves? In a study published in 2019, conducted by PsychTests, researchers compared two groups of people: one group that would admit when they'd made a mistake, and one that wouldn't. The study found that for the group who wouldn't acknowledge their faults, a significant majority (67 percent) of the participants "hate admitting they're wrong" and 68 percent have a "deep fear of rejection."[3] Admitting we're wrong comes with one of the most uncomfortable and avoided human emotions—shame. Shame is the feeling that follows the reckoning with not just what we've done but who we actually are. *Collins* defines *shame* as "the painful feeling arising from the consciousness of something dishonorable, improper, [or] ridiculous."[4] This definition gives us further insight into why people go to such great lengths to avoid it. Particularly the "painful" part that comes as a result of "consciousness." Author, professor, and "shame expert" Brené Brown has made a career studying and talking about shame. In a 2012 TED Talk she defines shame like this:

> Shame is a focus on self, guilt is a focus on behavior. Shame is *"I am bad."* Guilt is *"I did something bad."*
>
> How many of you, if you did something that was hurtful to me, would be willing to say, *"I'm sorry. I made a mistake"*? How many of you would be willing to say that? Guilt: I'm sorry. I made a mistake. Shame: I'm sorry. I am a mistake.[5]

In this talk Brené Brown put her finger on the real reason we fear our "What have I done?" moments. If we face what we've done, it will so often tell us just how bad *we* are. In an article from *Psychology Today*, psychotherapist F. Diane Barth says,

> Shame can lead us to hide our mistakes from others, which can be a highly destructive combination. Once you are hiding your mistakes, you not only don't learn from them, but often you make them worse, either through attempts to cover them up or through misguided efforts to correct them.[6]

It's clear that humans desire to hide from, ignore, and escape what they've done and who they are. But the real question is, *why?* The answer is shame, and as Brené Brown points out, shame is so painful because it tells us a difficult and ugly story of who we are, and if who we are is "bad," we stand to lose everything we desire and need most: acceptance, value, and love. So we do everything in our power to avoid what, I believe, we all know deep down is true about ourselves.

Prodigal

The first feature film I wrote and filmed was a modern retelling of the parable of the prodigal son, told by Jesus, called *Confessions of a Prodigal Son*. The story is about a young man who takes his father's money and moves to a far-off city where, through a series of selfish and rebellious choices, he finds himself living in a ruin of his own making. As a young and struggling artist who had gone to Hollywood to seek fame and fortune and had more than a handful of my own prodigal moments, regrettable decisions, and destructive outcomes, I strongly resonated with the story.

But the part of that beautifully told biblical narrative that struck me the deepest is when the Prodigal Son, after his world crashed in on him, found himself in the middle of his own "What have I done?" moment.

> When he finally came to his senses, he said to himself, "At home even the hired servants have food enough to spare, and here I am dying of hunger!" (Luke 15:17 NLT)

It's a short moment, written in the ancient and succinct style, but still, in those words in the context of the story, you can feel the deep and real pain the son experienced when finally acknowledging the reality of what he'd done, who he'd become, and where he'd ended up.

I wanted to make sure in my modern and semi-biographical iteration to capture the depths and importance of this necessary moment in my and the Prodigal Son's redemption stories. We shot the scene in a small motel, where I tried with all the ability I had to give a performance on camera that would capture the weight of a "What have I done?" moment. The movie is filled with flaws and imperfections, but that scene stands as one of my favorites as it strikes to the heart of one of the most important and meaningful steps toward experiencing redemption and healing.

Acknowledgment

One of my favorite paintings is a classic titled *Stańczyk*. Painted in 1862, the artist, Jan Matejko, depicts an eye- and mind-catching scene of a court jester dressed in a bright-red onesie complete with a bell-covered jester's hat. But this jester isn't performing, telling jokes, or smiling; instead he is distressed and slumped over in a wooden chair in a dark room, while behind him in the next room over, a lively party takes place. On the table next to the sad clown is a letter that, as the story goes, contains the devastating news that the kingdom he belongs to has lost a great battle, and the armies of the enemy force will soon be upon the partying castle's doors.

This painting so perfectly encapsulates what I've felt so many times when confronted with the dire situations that so many seem to be able to ignore and escape while I no longer can. Situations that make it impossible to ignore the depressing reality I have found myself in.

It's a hard thing, finding ourselves in a "What have I done?" moment, and it's a painful and scary thing to respond to them with "mea culpa," accepting our fault. But it's there, moving the rubble, darkness, and mess, that we inch our way toward a more beautiful life and the redemption our hearts so long for, the one God promises us.

> So I turned to the Lord God and pleaded with him in prayer and petition, in fasting, and in sackcloth and ashes.
>
> I prayed to the LORD my God and confessed:
>
> "Lord, the great and awesome God, who keeps his covenant of love with those who love him and keep his commandments, we have sinned and done wrong. We have been wicked and have rebelled; we have turned away from your commands and laws. We have not listened to your servants the prophets, who spoke in your name to our kings, our princes and our ancestors, and to all the people of the land.
>
> "Lord, you are righteous, but this day we are covered with shame—the people of Judah and the inhabitants of Jerusalem and all Israel, both near and far, in all the countries where you have scattered us because of our unfaithfulness to you. We and our

kings, our princes and our ancestors are covered with shame, LORD, because we have sinned against you. The Lord our God is merciful and forgiving, even though we have rebelled against him." (Daniel 9:3–9)

Chapter 9

DEATH AND RESURRECTION

Only birth can conquer death—the birth, not of the old thing again, but of something new. Within the soul, within the body social, there must be . . . a continuous "recurrence of birth" . . . to nullify the unremitting recurrences of death.

—Joseph Campbell, *The Hero with a Thousand Faces*

The first time I ever experienced death was when I was ten years old. A few years earlier, my siblings and I had begged our parents for a dog. After having been duly convinced, they presented us with a beautiful golden retriever puppy we named Penny. Penny was a dog that seemed almost like a character from a book or movie. She was more than a pet—she was a friend. She sat beside me on movie nights, snuggled with me while I did homework, and ran alongside me as I explored and played pretend on our land. She celebrated with a wagging tail when I returned home, and with a cocked head she tried to understand the words I said to her, comforting me with a gentle golden paw when my OCD became too overwhelming for my young brain to handle. Then one terrible day while we were on a family trip, my parents gathered us into their room. Before they said anything, I knew something wasn't right. Their faces were somber and hesitant. Then they gently told us the bad news, and like a boulder slamming into my young heart, I tasted the bitter reality of what death meant.

I didn't sleep that night. Instead I looked out a window through tear-fogged eyes and into a familiar night sky, and I spoke to God, asking him to do something. I wished and asked and pleaded to not let death be real for Penny. But it was real for Penny, and it's real for all of us.

The Hero's Journey

We all know the timeless and classic tale of Scrooge in Charles Dickens's *A Christmas Carol.* The main character is a cold and bitter man named Scrooge, who on the night before Christmas is visited by three spirits: one who shows him the past, another who shows him the present, and my favorite, the spirit who shows him the possible future. The Ghost of Christmases Yet to Come (the future spirit) is described as a haunting vision draped in a long black robe with a hood that hangs over the face of an unrecognizable black void.

In the greatest film adaptation of this story to date, *The Muppet Christmas Carol*, the Ghost of Christmases Yet to Come takes Scrooge, played brilliantly by Michael Caine, to a dark and empty graveyard in the middle of a bleak and chilly night. With his long and ominous hand, the spirit points to a gravestone, where engraved is Scrooge's name. This is Scrooge's "What have I done?" moment, a moment when suddenly he is confronted with the reality of his sins and the destruction they are causing, ultimately creating a future where he will die alone and despised. Scrooge drops to his knees in tears, buries his face in the folds of the spirit's robe, and with deep pain in his voice, begs him for another chance.

This scene of death is powerful and moving. But the story doesn't stop there. When Scrooge lifts his face from the robe of the spirit, he finds himself back in his room on Christmas morning, with light shining through the window and upon his tear-stained face. And while it seems that things are back to normal, Scrooge is a changed man. As a result of experiencing death, Scrooge finds himself resurrected into a new and more beautiful life.

The story that began with Scrooge heartlessly muttering "Bah humbug" ends with this:

> "I don't know what to do!" cried Scrooge, laughing and crying in the same breath. . . . "I am as light as a feather, I am as happy as an angel, I am as merry as a school-boy. I am as giddy as a drunken man. A merry Christmas to everybody! Happy New Year to all the world!"[1]

Joseph Campbell, in his seminal work *The Hero with a Thousand Faces*, writes about something called "the hero's journey." The hero's journey is map of similarities in structures and narratives that all the great tales have in common. This recipe of the hero's journey, this formula for good stories, is a circle that begins with elements like "the call to adventure" (the inciting incident) and "crossing the threshold" and ends with "revelation" and "atonement."[2] But right in the middle, right in the crux of every great story, is one of the most important phases of all: the death and resurrection moment.

The death and resurrection moment is when the hero experiences some kind of metaphorical or literal death before rising again to a new life. We see this in movies like *Star Wars*. At the end of *The Empire Strikes Back*, Luke Skywalker, after being defeated by Darth Vader, falls into a seemingly endless abyss, only to be brought back stronger ("resurrected") in the next film, *The Return of the Jedi*, to complete his destiny. We see it in books like *The Chronicles of Narnia* series, where Aslan, the creator of the world in *The Lion, the Witch and the Wardrobe*, allows himself to be killed by the dark forces, only to rise again and defeat the evil White Witch and destroy the curse she has placed over the whole world. We see it in video games, like the aptly named *Red Dead Redemption*, where John Marston, an outlaw who tries to change for the better, ultimately dies when the law catches up to him, only to be "resurrected" in the form of his son, Jack, becoming a good man.

In the critically acclaimed 2018 video game *Red Dead Redemption 2*, widely considered to be one of the greatest video games ever made, you play as Arthur Morgan against an epic backdrop of turn-of-the-century Wild West, with its golden fields, endless forests, and towering mountains. Arthur is a bad man who has spent the majority of his existence as an outlaw killing and stealing his way through life. But when his conscience is touched after a chance encounter with a nun at the beginning of his story, Arthur has his own "What have I done?" moment, and we follow him as he fights, claws, and stumbles his way toward some semblance of redemption. (Spoiler alert next.) But try as he might to make a new way and change his future, Arthur's past catches up with him and he faces death after contracting a deadly disease and running from old enemies out for his life. Toward the end of the story, Arthur again comes across the kind nun, and this heartbreaking but touching scene takes place.

Sister Calderón: What's wrong?

Arthur: I'm, uh . . . I'm dyin', Sister. Yeah, I got TB. I got it . . . beatin' a man, to death . . . for a few bucks. I've lived a bad life, Sister.

Sister Calderón: We've all lived bad lives, Mr. Morgan. We all sin . . . but I know you.

Arthur: You don't know me.

Sister Calderón: Forgive me, but that's the problem. You don't know you.

Arthur: What do you mean?

Sister Calderón: I don't know. Whenever we happen to meet, you're always helping people and smiling.

Arthur: I had a son. He passed away. I had a girl who loved me. I threw that away. My momma died when I was a kid, and my daddy . . . well, I watched him die. And it weren't soon enough.

Sister Calderón: My husband died a long time ago. Life is full of pain. But there is also love and beauty.

Arthur: What am I gonna do now?

Sister Calderón: Be grateful that for the first time, you see your life clearly. Perhaps you could help somebody. Helping makes you really happy.

Arthur: But . . . I still don't believe in nothin'.

Sister Calderón: Often, neither do I. But then I meet someone like you, and everything makes sense.

Arthur: Heh . . . You're too smart for me, Sister. I guess I . . . I'm afraid.

Sister Calderón: There is nothing to be afraid of. Take a gamble that love exists, and do a loving act.[3]

Not long after their talk, Arthur sacrifices his life to save the life of his friend and fellow outlaw John, who uses death as a catalyst to begin his own journey of redemption. Only through Arthur's death does his friend find new life.

But all these admittedly wonderful stories are only reflections of what Joseph Campbell realized was the greatest story ever told—the Christ story. In the life of Jesus we see the perfect example of what a story was made to be. And the crux of the Christ story is the brutal and awful death of God followed by his triumphant and beautiful resurrection. The followers of Jesus used his external death and resurrection as a picture of what God is able to do internally for each of us. Our hearts are wired to desire new life in the midst of the internal deaths (heartbreak, despair, hopelessness) that all of us experience. This is one reason Jesus's story continues to draw in and inspire billions, even two thousand years after it took place.

There's More!

The idea of the process of death and life is found not only in stories but in all of nature. A seed must break apart and "die" in the dark of soil for a flower to bloom in the light. There's a concept in science known as "apoptosis," which is essentially the process by which a cell dies so that new ones can be made.[4] Death and resurrection are programmed into our very cells and written on our souls.

It's all fine to see new life in nature or watch and read about resurrection in stories, but when we have our own "What have I done?" moment and find ourselves in a place of experiencing internal death, it hurts, a lot. The deaths we commonly experience are the death of our belief in our own goodness, the death of believing we deserve love, the death of dreams, the death of our abilities, the death of our self-worth. These deaths can be so unbearably painful and viscerally hurtful that often they cause us to wonder if redemption is even real and if resurrection from them is possible. Experiencing these internal deaths often proves too much for many of us, and instead of holding on to the hope of resurrection, or renewal, we instead find it impossible to see past the fog of despair and then sink into deeper depression, addiction, solitude, or even suicide. We often sink because we believe this death is the end and there's no hope to be found.

According to the American Foundation for Suicide Prevention, suicide is one of the leading causes of death.[5] On top of that, in 2020 the entire world experienced death all together, nearly all at once, in the form of the COVID-19 pandemic. While, sadly, the pandemic caused millions of physical deaths,[6] it also caused countless mental and emotional ones as people were suddenly cut off from their lives, friends, families, dreams, and distractions. Some of this was due to loneliness, fear of infection, grief after bereavement, and financial worries.[7]

But some of us were forced into our own moments of self-reflection, where we had to look at who we really were when many of the distractions of modern society were taken away. According to the American Foundation for Suicide Prevention, "depression is the most common condition associated with suicide."[8] And one of the most depressing things we can ever experience is the honest reckoning with our regretful failures and irreversible fractures.[9] This internal death can feel final, and too many people have believed the lie that this moment of death *is* final, that there's nothing after it, that it's the end of their story. But it's not. Thanks be to God, it's not, and there's more to your story.

Too many people have believed the lie that this moment of death *is* final. But it's not.

Joseph Campbell discovered that for stories to be great—ones worth telling, with weight and power—the main character must experience a death of some kind so that ultimately the hero can triumphantly move toward what is baked into reality—new life. It can be so hard to see our own stories objectively because we don't have that third-person perspective where we can see our story's timeline from up above and be comforted by the assurance that it'll all work out in the end. We're stuck in our current and often painful moment with no guarantee of a future with relief and redemption, no guarantee that the death we are experiencing will ever end. But we can see the stories of triumph from other people who have. And as I look through history at the greatest stories of redemption, one common factor in each of their narratives is their faith, their belief that whatever death they were experiencing was simply a necessary part of their tale that would—should they hold on, believe, and keep moving—result in new life.

New Life

I remember the night my parents found the pictures I had been looking at on the internet. I was a teenager and hadn't learned to delete my browsing history yet (which, by the way, cannot be fully deleted anyway). There in my living room, confronted with the reality of what I had done, I felt like I was falling through the floor, and that I'd never be able to crawl out of the abyss of guilt and shame that had swallowed me whole. My parents had been kind, offering help in love at the discovery of my hormonally guided misdeeds, but my mind had not offered me the same mercy. My obsessive-compulsive thoughts began playing on repeat. I had messed up too badly; I had gone too far. I had faced my own adolescent "What have I done?" moment, and it had pushed me into a dark and desperate place where I couldn't see how redemption was possible. I couldn't sleep that night; shameful thoughts raced through my head and covered me in a shadow I couldn't shake. I prayed and prayed, begging God for forgiveness just to experience some sort of solace. I looked out my second-story window, and for the first time in my short life, I wondered if I should jump out of it, as there was no hope left.

I made it through that night. And in the morning, when I saw the welcoming and loving smile on my mother's face in the new day's light, I suddenly found myself a new man—my mistakes were in the past. I felt the relief of no longer having to hide my sins, and I experienced the freedom of being a new person inside. I had made it through the dark of being faced with my own brokenness and into the light, where the world was bright and I was new.

A decade later I found myself facing another moment of death, when I sat in an empty apartment after a brutal divorce. One that brought a death of the future I had dreamed of, the image of what people thought of me, and a relationship I had put years of work into. I was embarrassed, ashamed, and heartbroken. And again the thought crossed my mind that this was the end, that there was nothing after this, that maybe I should put myself out of my misery. But I didn't. At that moment on an old couch in a lonely room, I asked God to be with me. As I did, I remembered all the moments of death I had experienced before, starting with the first time as a teenager all those years ago, then moving through a decade of disappointments, mental breakdowns, and regretful decisions. I remembered that no matter how dark and shadowed those moments were, there was goodness after them. I chose to believe what I couldn't see in that moment—that while having to exist for a time in the painful place the "What have I done?" moment brought me to, redemption and new life awaited. And they did.

And after that, I remember stepping up to the front of a long line beneath the soaring arches of a grand cathedral in New York City. The man at the altar dipped his finger into a silver tray of ashes and marked my forehead with a cross, saying the words that have been said every year to countless others for thousands of years. "From dust you have come and to dust you shall return."

As I walked home through the crowded city streets of New York City, sprinkled throughout the bustling crowd were individuals whose foreheads were adorned with the same ashen cross as mine.

As I write this, I am currently in Lent, the season in which every year tens of millions of Christians spend forty days remembering Christ's death. They do this by joining the universal church on Ash Wednesday to receive the cross of ashes on their foreheads as a visual reminder of the death the God of the universe endured. Then, in likeness to God, Christians join in the season of remembering death by giving something up, choosing to experience loss of some kind in the form of fasting—sometimes meat, sweets, cursing, video games, even social media.

To an outsider, I imagine it could look rather macabre watching an entire group of people spend more than a month thinking about death. But a central part of the Christian story is death. It's something we've come to be acquainted with in a way no other group has. The most recognizable symbol of Christianity is a cross, the instrument of death on which our God was crucified. And instead of hiding from this symbol of death, we hang it in the center of our places of worship, put it on the walls of our homes, and even wear it around our necks. I have a tattoo of a cross on my ribs.

But why do we do this? Why do we center our most deeply held beliefs around pictures of death—something, it seems, the rest of the world is desperate to ignore and escape?

After the forty days of Lent, the season ends on Easter, the holiday that suddenly gives context and completion to the season of death we endure every year. Easter is the day we celebrate God's triumph over death in his brilliant and beautiful resurrection, which in turn invites us into the celebration of the new life and resurrection he has promised all of us. So why do we Christians spend more than a month thinking about death, displaying and wearing objects of death? Because we know what comes after—new life. These moments and images of death are reminders that ultimately death doesn't win. That new life and resurrection await us on the other side of the crucifixions we experience.

Change Is Ahead

In my family home there's a framed picture of a verse written out in hand-crafted calligraphy, and the beauty of the letters and the intricate gold frame serve as an ironic juxtaposition to what the words actually say: "I DIE DAILY."

Admittedly, this was an interesting thing to have hanging outside my room growing up. And for years I didn't get what it meant, thinking it was out of place among the more encouraging and uplifting verses that covered the walls. But years later when I finally looked at the full context of what the Scripture writer said, it clicked. The author of Colossians, Paul, spent an entire section exploring figurative death—something we're all acquainted with in one way or another—and life—something we all long for. He ultimately expressed that we must die, that we must experience little crucifixions, a killing of the old things (the mistakes, fears, regrets, habits, and doubts) to experience the new life that God offers (Colossians 3:1–5). In this idea of dying daily, the author pointed to the importance of regularly choosing to put to death what we must leave behind so we can move toward the life that lies ahead (v. 5). And in 1 Corinthians 15, Paul provided a stunning picture of what awaits us on the other side of physical death: "We will all be changed—in a flash, in the twinkling of an eye, at the last trumpet. For the trumpet will sound, the dead will be raised imperishable, and we will be changed" (vv. 51–52).

And it's here that Paul pointed out something even more powerful: While resurrection and new life are possible, we aren't raised into the same life, into the same person we were before. We will be "changed"; we will be wholly new and different creatures. It's by death we are resurrected into something new.

In that same vein, crucifying our "anger, rage, malice" (Colossians 3:8) offers the untold beauty of peace, thankfulness, and wisdom (vv. 15–16).

Years ago I wrote a film script entitled *City of Night*, which is about the people who live in a city that has only ever known night. So when a mysterious stranger appears telling the people about a place of day, a place with light, each character must decide to either stay in the dark and decaying city or follow him outside the city walls to the hope of a better world that lies beyond the eternal night they've been living in.

I hope to make this movie one day in an effort to use this allegory to encourage people to believe that there is something beautiful just beyond the dark mess we've been living in. But it's only for those brave enough to look at and own up to the mess we've made and follow God to new life.

Redemption Arc

To be raised again, to be changed into something more beautiful and whole, is the hope and assurance we're given that satisfies the desire that lies in the heart of every human soul. Sooner or later, whether we like it or not, we will all experience the bitter taste of internal death that has woven itself through this broken world. Like physical death, internal death has a sting so painful that it can lead us to believe there is no hope beyond the moment of loss these crucifixions bring. But God came, died, and rose again to give us a picture of what he offers to us and what can be a reality in our stories. Death is not the end. Death is only one part of our redemption arc; it is merely the necessary interlude to our being raised, changed, and given new life. This redemption and resurrection, modeled first by God through his physical death and resurrection, is offered freely to us should we take it.

> But in fact, Christ has been raised from the dead. He is the first of a great harvest of all who have died. So you see, just as death came into the world through a man, now the resurrection from the dead has begun through another man. Just as everyone dies because we all belong to Adam, everyone who belongs to Christ will be given new life. But there is an order to this resurrection: Christ was raised as the first of the harvest; then all who belong to Christ will be raised when he comes back. (1 Corinthians 15:20–23 NLT)

Chapter 10

WHAT NOW?

The world is indeed full of peril and in it there are many dark places; but still there is much that is fair, and though in all lands, love is now mingled with grief, it grows perhaps the greater.

—J. R. R. Tolkien, *The Fellowship of the Ring*

I walked trepidatiously into the small office. The afternoon sun streaked through the shutters and over an empty couch that sat across from a chair occupied by a fit middle-aged man wearing a button-down, holding a pad and pen in his hand.

"Come in. Take a seat!" he said as I shut the door and walked to the couch.

Therapists' offices always seem to have the same familiar trappings, as if there's a therapists' interior design catalog they all shop from—tidy furniture, a bookshelf of psychiatry books, outdated magazines on small coffee tables, all pulled together by a lingering smell of Febreze. I'd been in and out of therapists' offices since I was a mentally ill kid, but it had been a few years since I had been back, after which I had grown to believe that, for the most part, I had my life under control. But recently I had entered a new relationship, a serious one, the first person I felt I could love since my divorce. And there's something about falling in love with someone else that makes us evaluate ourselves—it forces us to look more honestly upon all the inconvenient and uncomfortable truths about how our stories have affected who we are. Before her, I believed things were going fine. I believed I was fine. In fact, that's exactly what I would say when people would ask how I was: "Fine." I thought this because I had done the things I was supposed to do—read the right books, said the right prayers. I had mentally forgiven the ones who'd wronged me—my ex, the church, the world. I had even faced my mea culpa and learned to admit my own shortcomings and faults. Which was why it was such a surprise to find this new relationship had whipped me into a sudden and chaotic storm of being haunted by emotions, thoughts, fears, and destructive behaviors I believed I had long since conquered.

It became clear that if I was going to learn how to love and be loved again—to be healthy and whole—I needed help finishing the process I had no idea still needed to be finished. The narrative of my healing and redemption was only in the middle of a story that longed for completion. I had wrongly believed that by simply letting go of blame and owning up to my own faults, I was done. But I was learning that it was just the beginning of my redemption journey—the longer and much more difficult part of not just recognizing the broken pieces but actually working with God to put them back together.

I sat down across from the gentle-eyed man who I hoped could help me quickly assess, address, and fix my problems and then send me on my merry way.

"What can I help you with today?" He clicked his pen, inviting me to guide this conversation with my opening remarks.

I paused, unsure how much I should dump right away, not wanting to overwhelm the poor guy with a word-waterfall of trauma. But I also didn't want to waste time, and I trusted he knew what he was doing. So I let loose. I opened up and shared with a complete stranger what I had been through—detailing the most devastating moments of my journey. The pernicious and persistent dark thoughts. The insecurities, fears, and doubts.

And thus began the next and greatest part of my journey, walking toward redemption. It was not a quick journey, like I had hoped. It was a long and difficult one—one I'm still on—but filled with continuous and glorious new moments of freedom that usher me ever so slowly toward God's promised land of wholeness and freedom that still awaits me.

Getting Undressed

C. S. Lewis's classic book *The Voyage of the Dawn Treader*, from *The Chronicles of Narnia*, introduces us to an unlikable and unpleasant young boy named Eustace Scrubb, the main character. Throughout the course of the story, Eustace acts selfishly, behaves awfully, and blames constantly. He acts so badly that eventually he turns into a terrible fire-breathing dragon. Eustace doesn't realize what he's turned into at first, reveling in his own self-righteousness.

But soon the realization that he's become a monster falls upon him after he stops looking to blame others and gazes into a mirrored pool that reveals his hideous reflection. In this moment he suddenly realizes what he's done and what he's turned into. He has his mea culpa moment, and he admits he's the worst and is overcome with deep sadness. Eustace the dragon weeps at seeing the ugly reality his own choices have turned him into.

It's there in the midst of his tears that suddenly Aslan—his creator, a mighty lion—appears. He says he can turn Eustace into a human boy again, he can remake him, but he will have to "undress" him from the hard and sharp scales that have covered his body and heart, and it will hurt. Finally, in a place of desperation and admittance of his own need for help, Eustace agrees to let his creator go about the process of making him new again. Eustace describes the process of shedding his scales: "The very first tear he made was so deep that I thought it had gone right into my heart. And when he began pulling the skin off, it hurt worse than anything I've ever felt."[1]

This is a moving scene for any of us who have, like Eustace, made the difficult decision to look at our own darkness and finally have a face-to-face encounter with our Creator, who appears ready and willing to "undress" us from our own destructive and hardened scales. But while most theologians and literary critics focus primarily on the powerful moment of Eustace's salvation, I am equally as struck by what comes after. Once the scales have fallen from Eustace's skin and he is given his second chance, C. S. Lewis writes this:

> It would be nice, and fairly nearly true, to say that "from that time forth Eustace was a different boy." To be strictly accurate, he began to be a different boy. He had relapses. There were still many days when he could be very tiresome. But most of those I shall not notice. The cure had begun.[2]

In this quote we see that Aslan, the creator, didn't provide an ending to Eustace's story, but rather a beginning. "The cure had begun" shows us that our moment of salvation is simply the start to our long and difficult but eternally meaningful stories. "He began to be a different boy" is a powerful truth that we can see in our own lives after God has saved us from who we were—that we can begin to be a different person.

Canceling Ourselves

The renowned writer and therapist Dan Allender once wrote, "The work of restoration cannot begin until a problem is fully faced."[3]

I wrote this book you're reading in an attempt to help us (myself included) bravely face our problem, which just so happens to be ourselves. This book has explored the concept and methodology of canceling ourselves—tearing our gazes away from the problems of others and admitting our own faults, that we're the worst—for the betterment of our worlds and our individual selves.

We don't act out these practices as a way to end the process of experiencing redemption and wholeness but rather to begin it. Redemption is a lifelong journey we take with our Creator, one that begins with not wasting time finding the specks in others' eyes but instead learning the art of acknowledging the log in our own. But simply acknowledging the log isn't enough—we must then go about the difficult and often painful process of removing it, then taking the necessary and numerous steps to heal from the damage that living with a log in our eye has left.

In the same way, conversion is only the first step to living a life following Jesus. Ceasing our judgment of others, falling on our knees, and confessing our sins is simply the opening chapter to the rest of our book of redemption, one that will be a work of a lifetime. We live in an age of immediacy: We get our food, entertainment, and even sex with the swipe of a finger on our phones. We can lose weight instantly with shots and wipe out headaches with pills and fly across the world in a few hours. But the reality is, anything that's truly and lastingly good takes effort and dedication over a long period of time. Great stories don't happen in the first chapter—they happen over dozens. And our stories of redemption are no different.

New Path

There's a sad story in Matthew 19 about a rich young man who, upon hearing Jesus's words and messages, has a sudden flash of inspiration and desire to be a part of the eternal kingdom Jesus is talking about. He asks Jesus, "What good thing must I do to get eternal life?" (v. 16). After Jesus tells him to follow the Ten Commandments, the man tells Jesus he is a moral person and keeps the Ten Commandments, hoping (I think) that will be enough to get him in. Jesus, knowing the man's heart, tells him that to find eternal life, he needs to give up his riches and give to the poor, then follow him. Upon hearing this, the man despairs and walks away from Jesus's invitation for eternal life.

While there are many great lessons about the dangers of materialism to be found in this passage, I wonder if the reason the young man walked away from Jesus's offer wasn't just because he'd have to give up his nice stuff and loads of money but ultimately because he'd have to *follow* Jesus. *Follow* means "to engage in or be concerned with as a pursuit," which indicates a long period of time on a particular path.[4] It was no accident the rich man asked what "thing" (singular) he needed to do to get what Jesus offered—possibly indicating he was looking for a quick way, a momentary action, a single thing he could *do* to get what Jesus was promising, but in a way that wouldn't take much effort, time, or sacrifice.

Great stories don't happen in the first chapter—they happen over dozens. And our stories of redemption are no different.

While it's easy to judge that rich young man, we are guilty of this too. We have a proclivity to ignore Jesus's invitation to follow him and instead look for the silver bullets and magic beans that will give us what we most desire in an instant. We want what God has to offer us—healing, restoration, happiness, wholeness—but we want them now, without the trouble of giving our whole lives to find them. God's promises aren't destinations we can immediately arrive at but are instead journeys we take, beginning now and stretching into eternity.

You see, God is a God of process. He didn't write the stories in Scripture on a single page in a day but wove a tale spanning thousands of years. Flowers and trees go through a long, arduous process before they bloom. Humans begin as mere cells that transform slowly over nine months before they're ready to be birthed, and nearly three decades before the brain and adult bodies are fully developed.[5] Our stories of wholeness are no different—they will take time and effort and will require a God-created process to be completed (Philippians 1:6). That process is following Jesus.

To begin, we must first have an encounter with God, like the rich young man standing face to face with Jesus. Many of us spend so much of our lives avoiding or running from this encounter, attempting to find the healing we so desire in a million other places. But in canceling ourselves, recognizing our need, and admitting we're the worst, we allow ourselves to finally encounter a God who's been waiting for us. It's there, standing face to face with our Creator, that we will have to choose: begin the story he has for us to tell or walk away. But encountering Jesus isn't the end of our journey—it's the opportunity for beginning it.

My original movie *Bright Sky* illustrates this nicely. I play an outlaw, William, who is looking for redemption and comes in contact with a prostitute running from her past (played by my real-life love interest, Keelia Clarkson). Throughout the movie, the characters take the difficult and often fraught journey away from their pasts toward a new, beautiful, and whole future together. They each have to reckon with the reality of who they've been and what they've done. They each have their own "What have I done?" moment, and they each experience a death of their old self in hopes of finding the new. (Spoiler ahead!) Toward the end of the film, William is in jail at the hands of a crooked sheriff, and seeing no way out, he looks through the bars of his cell and talks to God:

> God, it's me again. Can you hear me? I know we don't talk much, and I'm sorry for that—that's my fault. I should've been talking to you the whole time. You saved me once, and I need you to do that again. I want to be a better man, and I promise you if you help me, I will be. This isn't for me, because I know I don't deserve it. I don't know what else to say. I just need your help, and I think I always have. Amen.[6]

And in that prayer of admittance—in that encounter he chooses to have with his Creator—William experiences the other side of redemption even though he's behind bars. He experiences the first taste of the new him. Soon after this prayer, William rises up and out of his cell, and he steps into a new life and an ongoing happy ending. It's not that he doesn't still have flaws and fractures, it's not that he's become perfect, but it's that he's now following a new path led by God. A path away from who he was, what he'd done, and where he'd been and into a new and beautiful future where he heads toward who he was always created to be. Through his prayer of admittance, he changed the path he was on, and in doing so, he changed his destination.

Go the Distance

As I walked into the therapist's office that day, I went in believing that since I'd had my moment of realization, I was done. I was healed. I was finished. But I left knowing my initial moment of salvation—my encounter with God in the midst of my rubble—was only the beginning of my redemption story as I followed my Creator into a new world and a new me.

This book was written in an effort to help us stop looking at other people and other things so we can finally have an encounter with our Creator and he can tear the scales from our eyes and skin. But when we finally stand face to face with Jesus—like the rich young man and like Eustace Scrubb—it is just the beginning of our story, not the end. It's there, in front of God, that we are given the invitation to begin our stories and follow him. If we follow him, we take our first steps in an eternal journey of redemption, purpose, and love. It's a path that takes dedication and a willingness to go the distance worthy of the invaluable and abundant life God offers us.

Admitting we're the worst is hard. It hurts, and it will take sacrifice. Tearing our gaze from the sins of the other to look at our own brokenness and experience our true need is a choice that many spend lifetimes running from. But the ones brave enough to look in the mirror of their heart will find themselves face to face with their Creator. It's there we are offered the eternally important choice to either walk away or follow him into a new life. It's up to us, but it all begins with us admitting "I'm the worst."

> We have stopped evaluating others from a human point of view. At one time we thought of Christ merely from a

human point of view. How differently we know him now! This means that anyone who belongs to Christ has become a new person. The old life is gone; a new life has begun! (2 Corinthians 5:16–17 NLT)

Afterword

THIS BOOK IS FOR YOU

As I sit here at my computer and look out on New York City as the day fades into night, I take my gaze from the rooftops to the now-completed manuscript I have been working on for two years. It's one I have written in multiple cities, in different seasons, and in a million moments. And as I read over it again, I find myself thinking back to when I began this book. I think about who I was and who I am now.

I'd like to think that in the process of writing on this topic and meditating on these timeless, spiritual, and practical truths, I've in some small way grown better at acknowledging my own brokenness. And I think there has been change. I'm still prideful, selfish, and prone to taking the specks out of others' eyes while ignoring the log in mine, but I have found I'm *somewhat* slower to judge, more able to consider context, and faster at admitting my own fault. And I see how this has enabled me not only to love others better and more fully but also to find my way more quickly to asking for and receiving the help and grace I need.

I began writing this book as an exploration of a phenomenon I saw in humanity's tendency toward judgmentalism, tribalism, unforgiveness, dehumanization, antagonization, condescension, and self-righteousness. It wasn't written as a self-help book from an author, philosopher, or professional who'd figured out the answer and was kindly bestowing wisdom to the ones who needed to learn. Rather it was written as a confessional and personal exploration from the perspective of someone dealing with these tendencies and trying to figure it out for himself. As you read this book, you may have found yourself—like I often have—thinking of someone else, someone who *actually* needs to read this. It's natural to read about a problem and think of the people in our lives who have it. But I hope you will realize that the entire point of *I'm the Worst* is that it's for you; it's for me; it's for all of us—not all of *them*.

Recently I was watching a TV show that revolves entirely around American politics. This show originally aired twenty-five years ago, and each episode focused on different, relevant-to-the-time issues of politics, religion, race, division, tribalism, and conflict. I was curious to see if the world had become better since the show first released—better at erasing dividing lines of tribes, better at offering one another grace and empathy, better at acknowledging our own part in the brokenness of the world. But as I scroll on social media, watch the news, and read blogs, I'm sad to report that the same problems that existed all those decades ago still exist today, often in worse condition. This does make me sad, and if I'm not careful, it can bring about a spirit of hopelessness.

But as I go back through Scripture and study the interactions with and life of Jesus, I'm struck by how different his strategy for changing the world is from mine. Jesus counterintuitively seemed uninterested with gaining influence over large or powerful organizations. He didn't involve himself in the culture-war arguments the masses of the day preoccupied themselves with, and he didn't seek and destroy opposing groups. Rather, Jesus spent most of his recorded time on earth talking to individuals. Individuals like you and me. He spent his precious, short hours sitting with prostitutes, conversing with tax collectors, having one-on-one conversations with his disciples, and reaching into one heart at a time.

There's nothing I'd like to see more than a large-scale change of culture away from the more base and destructive tendencies we've talked about in this book and toward a better and more beautiful way. And often in a world where we measure success by numbers (views, subscribers, likes, dollars, etc.), it can feel as if small change is meaningless. But Jesus, God of the universe and the most influential person in history, didn't think this was the way. It's great to desire whole world transformation, but in reality, it begins with one person at a time. It begins with my heart changing and your heart changing.

So this book isn't for "culture" or for the "world"—this book is for *you*, and it's my hope that it can be used as an imperfect conduit for God to reach in and touch your individual heart. I'd like this book to help change the world, but I'm more interested in it helping to change your world.

Don't wait for the tides of culture to shift to take hold of God's truth and accept his gift of a more beautiful, whole life on the other side of admitting "I'm the worst."

Acknowledgments

In a cliché but accurate fashion, I first want to thank God. I want to thank and acknowledge God for loving and offering me unending grace and mercy even after I have messed up over and over again. I don't deserve it, but it was in following and trusting him that I learned that the redemptive power of admitting the reality of who I am is met with his unending love.

I want to thank my amazing, beautiful, faithful, and loving wife, Keelia, for taking this journey with me. She has so gracefully loved and forgiven me through my many flaws in a way I never thought possible. Without her constant encouragement, countless cups of coffee, endless insights, and nonstop editing sessions, this book (and this man) would not be a possibility.

I want to thank my entire family for putting up with me screwing up, running my mouth, and causing trouble for more than three decades. It's through them I first learned the amazing reality of being loved in spite of my brokenness, and for that I will always be eternally thankful.

I want to thank my friend Lou for the countless pizza nights that facilitated conversations in which I explored the concepts in this book deeply and authentically without judgment and with lots of laughter.

I want to thank my *Overthinkers* podcast cohost, Joseph Holmes, who built a place with me where we can talk ad nauseam and have fun thinking deeply about so many of the things I explored in the pages of this book.

I want to thank my entire Saturday Night Movie Club, who helped me think well about stories to illustrate my points better than I could on my own by giving me access to so many great pictures, metaphors, and allusions.

Notes

Chapter 1: We're Not Good

1. This story about Gilbert Keith Chesterton is considered likely to have occurred by the society of G. K. Chesterton, though the organization admits no one has done the research needed to verify it. See "What's Wrong with the World?", Society of G.K. Chesterton, April 29, 2012, https://www.chesterton.org/wrong-with-world/.
2. Ben M. Tappin and Ryan T. McKay, "The Illusion of Moral Superiority," *Social Psychological and Personality Science* 8, no. 6 (August 2017): 623–31, https://doi.org/10.1177/1948550616673878.
3. "Half of Americans Believe They're the Best Person," Behold Retreats, May 6, 2021, https://www.behold-retreats.com/media/nearly-half-of-all-americans-believe-theyre-the-best-person-they-know.

Chapter 2: But What About Them?

1. "Social Media and the Brain," Center for Humane Technology, accessed September 29, 2025, https://www.humanetech.com/youth/social-media-and-the-brain. The Center for Humane Technology notes that conceit is a potential side effect to engaging in social comparison while viewing social media, as is the increased polarization of society.
2. Saint Augustine, *The Confessions of Saint Augustine*, trans. E. B. Pusey (Project Gutenberg, 2001), ebook, https://www.gutenberg.org/files/3296/3296-h/3296-h.htm.

3. Son Pham, "Gen Z Proves Celebrity Gossip Is in Its Peak Era. What's Next?," *Medium*, April 13, 2023, https://medium.com/@beyondson/gen-z-proves-celebrity-gossip-is-in-its-peak-era-whats-next-16b1062a70d4.
4. Eugene Kitney (@prkitney), "Don't Judge Someone Just Because They Sin Differently Than You Do. Quit shaming people who Sin differently than you," part of the meme series Things That Made Me Go, "Hhmmmm," February 14, 2025, https://www.instagram.com/prkitney/p/DGEOg3WR1X9/.
5. Ken Sande, "Judging Others: The Danger of Playing God (Part 2)," Christian Counseling and Educational Foundation, April 14, 2016, https://www.ccef.org/judging-others-danger-playing-god-part-2/.
6. Michael Hidalgo, "Why Are Christians So Judgmental?," *RELEVANT*, October 23, 2024, https://relevantmagazine.com/faith/why-are-christians-so-judgmental/.

Chapter 3: A Culture of Canceling

1. *The Crucible*, written by Arthur Miller, directed by Nicholas Hytner (20th Century Fox, 1996), Apple TV.
2. *Britannica*, "Cancel Culture," updated July 15, 2025, https://www.britannica.com/procon/cancel-culture-debate.
3. Maddie Abuyuan, "Back from the Brink: What PR Agents and Branding Experts Have to Say About Cancel Culture," *HuffPost*, November 9, 2023, https://www.huffpost.com/entry/cancel-culture-pr-branding_n_6545210ee4b01b2585839161.
4. Andrew Corsello, "Louis C.K. Is America's Undisputed King of Comedy," *GQ*, May 13, 2014, https://www.gq.com/story/louis-ck-cover-story-may-2014.
5. *Sincerely Louis C.K.*, written and directed by Louis C.K. (Louis C.K., 2020), Apple TV.
6. *Collins Dictionary*, "culture," accessed August 28, 2025, https://www.collinsdictionary.com/dictionary/english/culture.
7. "A Brief History of Fundamentalism," Shepherds Theological

Seminary, accessed January 24, 2025, https://shepherds.edu/a-brief-history-of-fundamentalism/.

8. "What Is Fundamentalism?," GotQuestions.org, accessed February 15, 2025, https://www.gotquestions.org/fundamentalism.html.
9. Some of the fundamentalist movement scandals have been covered in the four-part documentary *Let Us Prey: A Ministry of Scandals*, directed by Sharon Liese (Investigation Discovery, 2023). It can be viewed on various streaming platforms, including HBO Max, Prime Video, and PBS.
10. Candice Frederick, "Where We Lost the Thread on Cancel Culture," *HuffPost*, November 6, 2023, https://www.huffpost.com/entry/cancel-culture-collapsed_n_652eb99ee4b00565b621b032. See also John MacArthur, "The Decline of Fundamentalism," Grace to You, November 6, 2015, https://www.gty.org/library/blog/B151106/the-decline-of-fundamentalism.
11. For more information on actor-observer bias, see "How Observer Bias, Actor-Observer Bias, and Biases Can Affect How We Relate to Others," BetterHelp, updated February 14, 2025, https://www.betterhelp.com/advice/behavior/can-observer-bias-cause-problems-in-relating-to-other-people/.
12. Dr. David Kyle Foster, "What Did Jesus Write on the Ground?" *Crosswalk*, updated November 9, 2023, https://www.crosswalk.com/faith/bible-study/what-did-jesus-write-on-the-ground.html.

Chapter 4: Hero Worship

1. "Remembering Waco," Bureau of Alcohol, Tobacco, Firearms and Explosives (ATF), last updated May 14, 2018, https://www.atf.gov/our-history/remembering-waco.
2. Lesley Kennedy, "Inside Jonestown: How Jim Jones Trapped Followers and Forced 'Suicides,'" HISTORY, last updated May 28, 2025, https://www.history.com/articles/jonestown-jim-jones-mass-murder-suicide.

3. Angela Serratore, "What You Need to Know About the Manson Family Murders," *Smithsonian Magazine*, July 25, 2019, https://www.smithsonianmag.com/history/manson-family-murders-what-need-to-know-180972655/.
4. Rick Ross, "Watch Out for Tell-Tale Signs," *The Guardian*, May 27, 2009, https://www.theguardian.com/commentisfree/belief/2009/may/27/cults-definition-religion.
5. Ashlen Hilliard, "Understanding a Cult Leader," People Leave Cults, May 24, 2023, https://www.peopleleavecults.com/post/cult-leader.
6. David Foster Wallace, "This Is Water," 2005 Kenyon College commencement address, May 21, 2005, transcript, https://people.math.harvard.edu/~ctm/links/culture/dfw_kenyon_commencement.html.

Chapter 5: Tribes Versus Communities

1. *Jojo Rabbit*, directed by Taika Waititi (Fox Searchlight Pictures, 2019).
2. "Health Effects on Social Isolation and Loneliness," U.S. Centers for Disease Control and Prevention (CDC), May 15, 2024, https://www.cdc.gov/social-connectedness/risk-factors/index.html.
3. Elizabeth Dixon, "The Importance of Cultivating Community: Why We Need Each Other," *Psychology Today*, August 20, 2021, https://www.psychologytoday.com/us/blog/the-flourishing-family/202108/the-importance-cultivating-community.
4. *Our Epidemic of Loneliness and Isolation: The U.S. Surgeon General's Advisory on the Healing Effects of Social Connection and Community* (Office of the U.S. Surgeon General, 2023), https://www.hhs.gov/sites/default/files/surgeon-general-social-connection-advisory.pdf.
5. Rebecca Dolgin, "The Impact of Covid-19 on Suicide Rates," Health Central, updated May 14, 2021, https://www.healthcentral.com/condition/coronavirus/covid-19-suicide-rates.
6. Tori DeAngelis, "Young Adults Are Still Lonely, but Rates of Loneliness Are Dropping Overall," *Monitor on Psychology* 54,

no. 5 (2023), https://www.apa.org/monitor/2023/07/young-adults-lonely-pandemic.

7. *Collins Dictionary*, "tribalism," accessed August 28, 2025, https://www.collinsdictionary.com/dictionary/english/tribalism.
8. Arash Javanbakht, "The Politics of Fear: How It Manipulates Us into Tribalism," *Psychology Today*, March 23, 2019, https://www.psychologytoday.com/us/blog/the-many-faces-anxiety-and-trauma/201903/the-politics-fear.
9. *Collins Dictionary*, "community," accessed August 28, 2025, https://www.collinsdictionary.com/dictionary/english/community.
10. David M. Chavis and Kien Lee, "What Is Community Anyway?," *Stanford Social Innovation Review* (2015), https://doi.org/10.48558/EJJ2-JJ82.
11. I am using *tribe* in a general sense and not making any sort of statement about ethnic groups who use this term.
12. "Nero's Reign of Terror: How Christians Became Scapegoats for Rome's Problems," History Skills, accessed January 24, 2025, https://www.historyskills.com/classroom/ancient-history/nero-christians.

Chapter 6: Forgive Them, for They Know Not What They Do

1. Victor Hugo, *Les Misérables*, trans. Isabel F. Hapgood (Thomas Y. Crowell, 1887), https://www.online-literature.com/victor_hugo/les_miserables/. The Literature Network offers searchable online literature and has the entire text of *Les Misérables*.
2. Nadine Collier, quoted in "Representatives of Charleston Shooting Victims 'Forgive' Dylann Roof," *The Guardian*, June 19, 2015, https://www.theguardian.com/world/2015/jun/19/charleston-south-carolina-shooting-dylann-roof-victims-statements.
3. Don Von Drehle et al., "How Do You Forgive a Murder?," *TIME*, November 23, 2015, https://time.com/time-magazine-charleston-shooting-cover-story/.
4. Søren Kierkegaard, *Works of Love*, trans. Howard Hong and

Edna Hong (Harper & Row, 1926), 247, https://openlibrary.org/books/OL19845701M/Works_of_love.

5. *The Britannica Dictionary*, "justice," accessed January 4, 2025, https://www.britannica.com/dictionary/justice.
6. *The Britannica Dictionary*, "revenge," accessed January 4, 2025, https://www.britannica.com/dictionary/revenge.
7. "Forgiveness: Your Health Depends on it," John Hopkins Medicine, accessed January 5, 2025, https://www.hopkinsmedicine.org/health/wellness-and-prevention/forgiveness-your-health-depends-on-it.
8. Judith Orloff, "The Power of Forgiveness: Why Revenge Doesn't Work," *Psychology Today*, September 8, 2011, https://www.psychologytoday.com/us/blog/emotional-freedom/201109/the-power-forgiveness-why-revenge-doesnt-work.

Chapter 7: Canceling God

1. *The Apostle*, written and directed by Robert Duvall (October Films, 1997), Apple TV.
2. *Don't Know Jack*, written and directed by Nathan Clarkson (independently distributed, 2022), Tubi.
3. Stephen Fry, "Stephen Fry on God | The Meaning Of Life | RTÉ One," interview by Gay Byrne, posted January 28, 2015, by RTÉ, YouTube, https://www.youtube.com/watch?v=-suvkwNYSQo.
4. Epicurus, quoted in Christopher Hitchens, *God Is Not Great: How Religion Poisons Everything* (Twelve, 2007), 268.
5. Jeffrey M. Jones, "U.S. Church Membership Falls Below Majority for First Time," Gallup, March 29, 2021, https://news.gallup.com/poll/341963/church-membership-falls-below-majority-first-time.aspx.
6. "Modeling the Future of Religion in America," Pew Research Center, September 13, 2022, https://www.pewresearch.org/religion/2022/09/13/modeling-the-future-of-religion-in-america/.
7. "Church Dropouts Have Risen to 64%—but What About Those

Who Stay?," Barna, September 4, 2019, https://www.barna.com/research/resilient-disciples/.
8. Carey Nieuwhof, "7 Ways to Respond to the Epidemic of Deconstruction," *Outreach Magazine*, May 23, 2022, https://outreachmagazine.com/features/leadership/71348-7-ways-to-respond-to-the-epidemic-of-deconstruction.html.
9. *Britannica*, "Problem of Evil," by Patrick Sherry, updated September 24, 2025, https://www.britannica.com/topic/problem-of-evil.
10. *Britannica*, "Problem of Evil."
11. Lee Strobel, "Handling Christianity's Toughest Challenge: Why Does God Allow Suffering?," Christian Research Institute, April 22, 2009, https://www.equip.org/articles/why-does-god-allow-suffering/.
12. Linda Lyle, "The Image of God: 'Imago Dei,'" Chrisitanity.com, updated August 13, 2025, https://www.christianity.com/wiki/bible/image-of-god-meaning-imago-dei-in-the-bible.html.
13. See 1 Timothy 2:4; 2 Peter 3:9; Isaiah 30:21; John 7:17.

Chapter 8: What Have I Done?

1. "Confiteor: A General Confession of Sins," Catholic Answers, accessed February 10, 2025, https://www.catholic.com/encyclopedia/confiteor.
2. *Collins Dictionary*, "mea culpa," accessed August 28, 2025, https://www.collinsdictionary.com/dictionary/english/mea-culpa.
3. "It Wasn't My Fault: New Study Looks at Why People Hate Admitting Mistakes," PsychTests, August 10, 2019, https://www.prweb.com/releases/it-wasn-t-my-fault-new-study-looks-at-why-people-hate-admitting-mistakes-801342370.html.
4. *Collins Dictionary*, "shame," accessed August 28, 2025, https://www.collinsdictionary.com/dictionary/english/shame.
5. Brené Brown, "Listening to Shame," TED Talk, Long Beach, California, March 2012, 20 min., 21 sec., transcript posted February 27, 2016, https://www.ted.com/talks/brene_brown_listening_to_shame.

6. F. Diane Barth, "It's Hard to Admit Mistakes: Here's Why You Should Anyway," *Psychology Today,* March 28, 2021, https://www.psychologytoday.com/us/blog/off-the-couch/202103/its-hard-to-admit-mistakes-heres-why-you-should-anyway.

Chapter 9: Death and Resurrection

1. Charles Dickens, *A Christmas Carol* (Bradbury & Evans, 1858), 92.
2. Joseph Campbell, *The Hero with a Thousand Faces*, 3rd ed. (New World Library, 2008), 210.
3. Scene from the end of *Red Dead Redemption 2,* played on PlayStation 4, released October 26, 2018, Rockstar Games.
4. National Human Genome Research Institute, "Apoptosis," updated September 29, 2025, https://www.genome.gov/genetics-glossary/apoptosis.
5. "Suicide Statistics," American Foundation for Suicide Prevention, updated April 1, 2025, https://afsp.org/suicide-statistics/.
6. "Global Excess Deaths Associated with COVID-19, January 2020–December 2021," World Health Organization, May 2022, https://www.who.int/data/stories/global-excess-deaths-associated-with-covid-19-january-2020-december-2021.
7. "COVID-19 Pandemic Triggers 25% Increase in Prevalence of Anxiety and Depression Worldwide," World Health Organization, March 2, 2022, https://www.who.int/news/item/02-03-2022-covid-19-pandemic-triggers-25-increase-in-prevalence-of-anxiety-and-depression-worldwide.
8. "Risk Factors, Protective Factors, and Warning Signs," American Foundation for Suicide Prevention, accessed January 26, 2025, https://afsp.org/risk-factors-protective-factors-and-warning-signs/.
9. Judith Johnson et al., "Resilience to Emotional Distress in Response to Failure, Error or Mistakes: A Systematic Review," *Clinical Psychology Review* 52 (March 2017): 19–42, https://doi.org/10.1016/j.cpr.2016.11.007.

Chapter 10: What Now?

1. C. S. Lewis, *The Voyage of the Dawn Treader* (HarperCollins, 2005), 116.
2. Lewis, *Voyage of the Dawn Treader*, 120.
3. Dan Allender, *The Wounded Heart* (NavPress, 2018), 12.
4. *Collins Dictionary*, "follow," accessed August 28, 2025, https://www.collinsdictionary.com/dictionary/english/follow.
5. Anne Jacobson, "When Is the Brain Fully Developed? Later than You Might Think," GoodRx, August 1, 2022, https://www.goodrx.com/health-topic/neurological/when-is-the-brain-fully-developed.
6. *Bright Sky*, written by Nathan Clarkson, directed by Spencer Folmar (BMG-Global, 2025).

Study Guide

The following study guide was written to help facilitate further thought and reflection on the themes and messages of the book. There is a short summary of each chapter followed by five probing questions that are meant to help tie the ideas together and encourage personal introspection on the topics raised in *I'm the Worst*.

This study can be done in a group setting—small group, book club, church study, or friend group—or it can be utilized for individual study alongside a journal. But no matter what the context, the hope is that this study will provide deeper thought, meditation, and ultimate change in the hearts and minds of those who read the book.

Chapter 1: We're Not Good

In chapter 1, Nathan introduces the main themes and explores why so many of us, after identifying the problems in the world, blame anyone and everyone but ourselves. We all see that there are terrible and awful things in the world, but when it comes to discovering who's to blame, we seem to have a blind spot for our tribes (political parties, religions, genders), our groups (our friends and family), and mostly ourselves. Through the use of stories and stats, Nathan establishes that this is very human. But he also goes on to claim that this practice of seeing the problems of others while ignoring our own keeps the world and ourselves from getting better and ultimately only causes the fracture to grow. Admitting our own faults and looking at our own flaws before those of others is a practice that God asks of us but is one that few of us are willing to do. It is a vital and worthy task to recognize our own faults. But it's also difficult to shake ourselves out of the culturally normalized practice of blaming others while ignoring our part in the brokenness of the world.

Discussion Questions

1. Do you think Nathan is correct in his evaluation of people's proclivity to see others as the problem while ignoring their own part in the fracture in the world?
2. Why do you think people go to such lengths to avoid seeing their own issues?
3. Why has avoiding our failures become such a normal practice, both throughout history and in today's culture?
4. Do you find it easier to recognize the faults of others than your own?
5. Do you blame others for the bad in the world more quickly than you own your part, no matter how small, in the darkness in the world?

Chapter 2: But What About Them?

In chapter 2, Nathan builds on the themes found in chapter 1 but focuses even more directly on the way we avoid our own issues by comparing ourselves to others (in a way that makes us look good and the others . . . not so good). We live in a world where we daily compare ourselves to those around us to feel better about ourselves, using a myriad of metrics—followers, likes, dollars, romantic partners, experiences, and many more. But we compare ourselves morally to others as well, utilizing a what-about-them mental strategy to focus on the sins of others as a way to not look at our own. It's natural to try to feel better about our own shortcomings by identifying something worse in someone else—even children use this tactic in attempts to shift blame, with cries of "But what about them?" The question remains: Is it a good and helpful thing to do this? And if not, what will happen if we keep doing it? Nathan suggests this practice will not only deepen divides between us and others by fanning the flames of antagonism and separation but will also keep us from addressing our own issues in need of attention, which grow more destructive over time. The longer we keep our critical gaze locked outward on others, the more we get in the way of our own healing.

Discussion Questions

1. Do you agree with Nathan that we live in an age of comparison? If so, what are some ways you compare yourself to others, and what motivates you to do this?
2. Do you believe you are better than some people? If so, what people or groups do you find yourself feeling superior to? What makes you believe that you are?
3. What do you believe to be the negative outcomes of comparing yourself to others, especially when done to feel better about yourself?
4. Have you noticed that when you compare yourself to those you believe are worse than you in some way, you simultaneously tend to ignore your own issues?
5. What are some ways you can practice taking your gaze off the sins and faults of others and turning it inward to evaluate yourself and your own behaviors, thoughts, motivations, and struggles?

Chapter 3: A Culture of Canceling

In chapter 3, Nathan takes a look at the ancient practice of permanently and publicly condemning someone for their sins, which has been repackaged in modern times as "cancel culture." Nathan posits that cancel culture is a natural product of what we read about in chapter 2, when we compare ourselves to others for the purpose of feeling better about ourselves. The permanency of cancel culture (utilizing a mob mentality to publicly and lastingly remove someone from society) can feel right and cathartic, dividing the "good" people from the "bad." Especially when we assume we are the "good" people. But the multiple unforeseen consequences of normalizing a puritanical and moralistic judgment of others is that while creating in us a self-righteousness, it doesn't actually help people become more moral. Instead, it teaches them only to appear and act moral while enabling them to never deal with the actual root issues. It also creates a culture of fear that the cancel gun could, at any minute, be pointed at us, causing us to live with a subliminal suspicion of others, which has a destructive effect on our hearts, heads, and relationships. But worst of all, with its permanent condemnation, cancel culture flies in the face of God's message of redemption, forgiveness, and new life.

Discussion Questions

1. Do you think cancel culture is a good thing or a bad thing? What are the positives, and what are the potential drawbacks?
2. Are there sins you identify as worse than others? Are there people you think are worse than others? Do you think some people should be cut off without the possibility of redemption?
3. Have you ever done something that you think makes you eligible for being canceled?
4. While holding people accountable for their actions is important, do you think there should be opportunity for redemption through true repentance? What should that process look like both publicly and personally?
5. Does God permanently cancel people without the possibility for redemption? How do you think God feels about his children canceling his children?

Chapter 4: Hero Worship

In chapter 4, Nathan takes us into the concept of hero worship and how our God-created design to worship and adore someone leads us to hold them up as figures to follow, love, and emulate. We see this in children as they learn to adore superheroes and pop stars, and we see this in adults as they give their hope and allegiance to pastors and politicians. This inclination was programmed in us to draw our gaze to God, but in our broken world we often look to insufficient alternatives. In the same way we can be blind to our own flaws and failures, we can also be blind to the reality of our heroes, figures, and leaders, who are ultimately just broken and flawed people themselves. They are poor counterfeits receiving our adoration and allegiance that should be given to the only person worthy of our worship and trust—God. When we put our hope and trust in counterfeit heroes and are blind to their human brokenness, we open ourselves up to being manipulated, used, and hurt, like we've seen in countless situations throughout history in cults, political movements, and prideful pastors. But we also make ourselves susceptible to distrust—after our trust is broken over and over again, we no longer believe anyone or anything, even God. Longing for heroes is a good, natural, and God-given instinct every human has encoded in their hearts and minds, but if it's not aimed at Jesus, we will be left hurt and even more broken.

Discussion Questions

1. Who was the first hero or figure you looked up to and were drawn to trust and/or emulate?
2. Has your desire to look to and trust a leader ever let you down? Have you been hurt before by someone you thought was worthy of following? What happened, and how did it affect you?
3. Why do you think humans have this natural inclination to lionize, trust, and follow a leader or figure?
4. What ways do you see people today putting their trust in leaders? Who are the leaders or figures you see people being drawn toward and following? Do you see this as a good or a bad thing? What are the potential drawbacks?
5. What makes God worthy of being followed? What are the benefits of worshiping, following, and trusting God?

Chapter 5: Tribes Versus Communities

In chapter 5, Nathan takes a deeper look at our human and God-given need for connection to other people and how that can lead us to healthy collectives—in the form of communities—or toxic ones—in the form of tribes. Nathan parses out the main differences between the two groups. Tribes are often built out of an antagonistic reaction to others in the world. They exist only in being against something or someone. They form out of fear and self-preservation, and they live at odds with any person or group that they identify as different from them, thus a threat to their existence and survival. Communities, however, are created out of shared mutual love. They are less occupied with identifying and finding protection from perceived outside threats and are more concerned with cultivating interior health through support. They are inherently more accepting and welcoming, not fearing others but rather inviting them to take part in the life they have built and the direction they are going. Being in a tribe makes us live in constant fear and antagonism. Living in community allows us to be in a context of mutual support and joy. Jesus, in his time on earth, rejected being a part of or forming his own tribe but rather used his life and ministry to build a community that focused on love, forgiveness, redemption, and joy. We know this community as the kingdom of heaven and see it lived out on this earth in the image of the church.

Discussion Questions

1. In seeing the difference between tribes and communities, it's easy to say that we prefer communities. But consider the aspects of tribes that you may be drawn to. Are some of the characteristics of a tribe appealing? Why?
2. Have you been, or are you, a part of a tribe (political, ideological, religious, etc.) that exists in reaction to and in fear of other groups or individuals? How has this affected you?
3. Have you been, or are you, part of a healthy community that was, or is, centered around mutual love and support? What are the positives you've seen from being a part of that kind of group?
4. What are the tribes you see most often today? Why do they exist, and what causes people to be a part of them? What is the result of their existence in culture and on individuals?

5. What do you believe God had in mind for human groups and connection? In thinking of how Jesus talked about and lived out the idea of the kingdom of heaven that the church should reflect, what should our groups look like?

Chapter 6: Forgive Them, for They Know Not What They Do

In chapter 6, Nathan broaches the difficult and often confusing topic of forgiveness. Forgiveness as a concept is one that most people agree is a good thing, but throughout the chapter, through reliable studies and personal and cultural anecdotes, Nathan shows just how hard it actually is for most of us to choose. Forgiveness can feel like we're letting people off the hook for terrible offenses, the world remains out of order, and we are expected to bear the pain of the fracture and accept it. We long for justice while still knowing we *should* forgive. It feels as though forgiveness would negate the justice God also says he cares about. This has created in our world and hearts an incorrect view of justice, which in turn becomes vengeance. And vengeance, no matter how good it feels in the short term, will eventually eat us alive and destroy us from the inside out. So it seems we're left with a choice either to be hurt by wrongdoers and do nothing, or to exact our own revenge, which only serves to deepen the brokenness already in the world. But Jesus, who preached about the necessity of both justice and forgiveness, gives us another way to interact with the wrongs committed against us. The first is realizing that *we* are in need of forgiveness and have already received it from God, if we chose to accept it. Remembering that we are recipients of his mercy allows us to more readily offer it to others. The second is that justice and forgiveness are not mutually exclusive and can work in tandem.

Discussion Questions

1. Have you ever chosen to forgive someone and felt that you had to ignore the consequences of their destructive actions? What did that feel like?

2. Have you ever needed forgiveness in a meaningful way and were either given it or not? What did that do for or to you?
3. Do you think we should always forgive, no matter what? If not, what are the times or situations you believe we shouldn't offer forgiveness?
4. What is the difference between justice and vengeance? What are some examples from fictional stories, history, or your personal life?
5. How can we both forgive and seek justice at the same time? How would that be practically lived out both culture-wide and in your own life?

Chapter 7: Canceling God

In chapter 7, Nathan explores the issue of anger and frustration with God for the bad things that happen in our world and our own lives. Which one of us hasn't wanted to shake our fists at God for the terrible things that have happened to us? Especially when we are told that God is all loving and all powerful. It seems that if he has the power to stop bad things from happening to us and others but doesn't, he must not love us. But if he *does* love us yet doesn't have the power to stop bad things from happening, he must not be God—or at least not the God that's as powerful as he's told us he is. It's an age-old question. Nathan believes it's also the number one reason people choose not to put their faith in God. So it's an important question that all too often is not validated by spiritual leaders and the church as a whole. Nathan contends that there is a logical and emotionally fulfilling answer—that God is entirely powerful, but because he respects our free will, he allows us to make decisions that hurt ourselves and others. And because he cares about our pain, he not only incarnated—came to earth—to be with us and experience the pain we feel, but also he offers us an eternity in a coming new world where all the pain and hurt we've experienced from a broken world will be undone.

Discussion Questions

1. Have you ever been angry at God for the bad things that happen in the world or in your own life? Have you wondered why he allows bad things to happen if he is all powerful and all loving?
2. Have you ever prayed and spoken to God about your frustrations or confusion with how he works or doesn't?
3. Do you believe God can be all powerful and all loving and still allow terrible things to happen? If so, how can both be true at the same time?
4. Do you believe the brokenness in the world is a result of God's choices or ours?
5. When have you experienced God's comfort in the midst of something painful that happened in your life? How did you see and experience his care and strength?

Chapter 8: What Have I Done?

In chapter 8, Nathan brings up a necessary step to the beginning of our redemption story. It's the moment when we realize what we've done, who we actually are, after we stop looking at the sins of others and turn our gaze inward to look upon our own fractures, flaws, and faults and the wreckage they have caused. This can be a particularly painful moment, one many people spend their whole lives running from instead of facing. Nathan calls it the "What have I done?" moment. He makes the case that it's a difficult but necessary encounter in the story of becoming whole and healed. It's a dramatic moment that appears in many great stories, films, and books and is often the catalyst to a character making necessary changes. This essential moment can bring about shame and self-hatred, which is natural, but it can also open a path to a new life. The act of looking at yourself and your destructive choices can hurt, but only when you survey the damage and the problem can you put the pieces back together and start the process of becoming who you were meant to be. This moment is one that God invites us into, but he doesn't leave us alone in the rubble of our mistakes. Rather, like a surgeon, he helps us identify the sickness and leads us out of our brokenness into wholeness and health. No one wants to admit they've messed up, but it's only through being brave enough to admit our faults that they can ever be fixed.

Discussion Questions

1. Have you ever found yourself trying to avoid or run from an uncomfortable truth or the consequences of your actions? Why? What happened as a result?
2. Have you ever had your own "What have I done?" moment, where you either chose or were forced to look at your mistakes, flaws, and failures and how they affected you and the world around you? What did you feel when that happened?
3. What are some "What have I done?" moments in either movies, books, or stories that are particularly heartbreaking and effective? What happened to the characters after they experienced them?
4. Do you think recognizing your own faults and failures is necessary to the process of becoming healed and whole? Why or why not?
5. Do you truly believe that God is inviting you to acknowledge your faults not to hurt you but to help you? How does God help us when we own up to our mistakes?

Chapter 9: Death and Resurrection

In chapter 9, Nathan talks about what comes after the "What have I done?" moment. After we make the decision to turn away from our judgment of others and gaze upon our own brokenness, what follows is a kind of death. Death of pride, death of ego, death of self-deception, death of self-righteousness, death of the untrue story we had been telling ourselves about ourselves. And this moment can be devastating and feel final. But the death we experience doesn't have to be the end of our story. If we choose to, it can be a new beginning. When this death occurs, it's then we have a choice to let that death destroy us and stay there in the ashes, or we can accept God's gift and rise to a new life. Death and resurrection are an integral part of the story God is telling in the world, beginning with the life, death, and resurrection of Jesus. But the concepts of death and resurrection also appear in the countless iterations within the greatest stories ever told on page, screen, or stage. Death and resurrection seem to be encoded in our hearts and minds, as if we were created by God to long for and seek it out. But the life we are resurrected into isn't the same one—it's a new life. This is good news. Death serves as a transforming element that, when passed through, changes us into something new. Something more whole and healed than we were before. So the death of our past selves isn't something to be feared but rather utilized to bring about the new people God created us to be.

Discussion Questions

1. Have you ever experienced a death of self in some way? A death of ego, pride, self-righteousness, etc.? How did it feel?
2. Have you experienced a new life of some sort as the result of something else dying? What was it?
3. Do you believe that to find new life there must be some sort of death? What does that look like practically in your life?
4. Why does something dying have the power of transformation? What is an example of transformation you have seen or experienced?
5. Aside from the Christ story, what are some of your favorite stories of death and resurrection, as they pertain to becoming a changed person, found in books, movies, or elsewhere?

Chapter 10: What Now?

In the tenth and final chapter, Nathan looks back at the journey of ideas and concepts explored throughout the pages of *I'm the Worst*. After having offered insight into taking our eyes off the sins of others, examining ourselves, evaluating our heroes, discovering what true community is, learning to forgive, experiencing our "What have I done?" moments, and embracing life after death, Nathan looks forward to how we should proceed in our stories with our newly found life. It's easy to believe that a new realization is just a temporary occurrence that lasts no longer than the moment it takes place. But Nathan argues that finding a new way of life with a new perspective is one we must choose every day, as each choice takes us one step further in the story that God has written for us to tell. The farther we walk on this path, the more we will see our own worlds change, which will bring about change in the larger world. It's easy to make a choice once, but to make it again and again is a more difficult—but ultimately more beautiful and rewarding—method. After reading this book, you haven't completed a course or finished a concept but rather have begun your journey with God into an eternal story.

Discussion Questions

1. Do you feel that you have understood and grasped the concepts explored in the book? Which ones most resonated with you? How will this affect the way you live from here on out?
2. Do you feel the necessity to practice the concepts from the book by making choices to accept the reality of yourself so that God can continue to work in your heart and mind? Why or why not?
3. How do you feel about the main theme of admitting your flaws, failures, and fractures? Do you agree with the premise and concept? Why or why not?
4. What practical changes are you ready to make in your life going forward, having to do with the themes of the book?
5. What are your final thoughts and reflections on the main theme? How do you feel about the concepts explored? What would you add to or subtract from Nathan's ideas?

NATHAN CLARKSON is an award-winning film and television actor, *Publishers Weekly* best-selling author, Netflix-trending filmmaker, and Spark Award–winning podcast philosopher. His books include *Different*, *Good Man*, and *Uniquely You*. As the cohost of *The Overthinkers*, he explores faith, art, philosophy, pop culture, and the big questions of life. He is a Patheos columnist at Cross Cultural, and he's been featured and quoted in the *Los Angeles Times*, *Variety*, *The Gazette*, *Publishers Weekly*, *World*, *Relevant*, and *Religion News Service*. Nathan and his wife, actress and novelist Keelia Clarkson, live between the streets of New York City, the lights of Los Angeles, and the mountains of Colorado Springs.

---

nathanclarkson.me

@nathanjclarkson

@nathanclarksoncreations